THE JOURNAL OF
THE CODY FIREARMS
MUSEUM

VOLUME IV • NUMBER 2
1993

BUFFALO BILL HISTORICAL CENTER
CODY, WYOMING

Library of Congress Number: 93-74797

International Standard Book Number. 0-931618-50-9

© 1993 by the Buffalo Bill Historical Center. All rights reserved.

Armax is published semi-annually by the Cody Firearms Museum, Buffalo Bill Historical Center, P.O. Box 1000, Cody, Wyoming, 82414, U.S.A. All correspondence concerning this journal should be directed to the above address.

Editor: Suzanne G. Tyler

Printed by Artcraft Printers, Billings, Montana, U.S.A.

THE SHARPS RIFLE IN FRONTIER MONTANA

by Gerald R. Mayberry

The September 17, 1881 issue of Miles City, Montana Territory's *Yellowstone Journal* reported the finding of a skeleton of a white man. Alongside the skeleton was a rusty Sharps carbine, still at full cock. It was impossible to tell if the weather, Indians or some other unknown danger had caused his death. In early-day Montana, even the possession of a Sharps carbine was not always enough to insure survival.

Sharps rifles were manufactured from 1849 to the early 1880s, a period which closely parallels Montana's history from a largely unexplored wilderness in 1850, to a separate territory in 1864, to a state in 1889. During this period, a transition also took place in the arms world, from muzzle-loader, to breech-loader, to repeater, to the eve of smokeless powder.

The Sharps rifle was arguably the best of the early breech-loaders. Furthermore, the continued development of a falling-block breech-loader combined with the introduction of metalic cartridges helped the Sharps rifle compete with later designs. Although not a repeater, it would for a time become the standard of power, range, accuracy and reliability, qualities that were especially desirable on the frontier. Many serious hunters would only have a Sharps rifle. In the case of the professional buffalo hunter, its use was virtually universal.

The romance of the Montana Sharps continues today. True Montana Sharps rifles remain in demand and may bring a premium when sold. Interest remains so high that five firms in Montana build or plan to build replicas. The Sharps is often depicted in the art of Montana painters, from Charlie Russell to the modern works of Ralph Heinz and Fred Fellows.

The first recorded use of a Sharps in what would become Montana was by the Isaac D. Stevens surveying party in 1853. Stevens later wrote, "The Sharps rifles issued . . . proved excellent and reliable arms."[1]

H.E. Dimick and Co. of St. Louis were soon advertising Sharps rifles that could be "loaded on horseback at a smart gallop, or lying down in the grass . . . Two hundred balls can be shot . . . in less time than with any other military or hunting rifle on this or 't'other side of Jordan. We will back our judgment with the 'filthy lucre' . . . that they are the best guns for persons exposed to the dangers of frontier life."[2] No doubt many who came to Montana around this time would bring a Sharps across the prairie or up the Missouri River.

Worman and Gavaglia, however, felt that "the gas-sealing devices in the Sharps percussion rifles worked well only as long as powder charges did not exceed 60 grains or so. The front-loading guns were [however] painfully slow to recharge."[3]

Early in Montana history, a Sharps rifle was used on the Yellowstone Expedition of 1863, led by James Stuart. The party left Bannock in early April of 1863, with plans to meet at a pre-arranged rendezvous site. The party was slow to arrive, due to the effects of Jim Gammall's "Minie Ball Whiskey." The party included 15 men, among whom were S.T. Hauser, later a prominent banker, and George Ives, who would be hung a year later by vigilantes among whom James and Granville Stuart would be counted as members.[4]

Three days after their departure, seven more men reached the rendezvous. This second party went on to discover the greatest gold strike in Montana history. This discovery, near what would become Virginia City, would play a large part in the creation of Montana Territory in 1864.[5]

Several days into the trip, the Stuart party met a Bannock village. With them was the Paiute medicine-man, Winnemucca, whom the Bannocks seemed to treat with respect and even fear, as he supposedly could make game plentiful or scarce, make one invulnerable to firearms and even catch a rifle ball in his hands. James Stuart's comment was, "I think he would have warm work stopping a ball from my trusty Sharps' rifle."[6]

The Bannocks held a scalp dance over seven fresh Flathead scalps. Stuart noted that "[s]uch is war among Indians. A massacre of the weak and defenseless by the strong, as opportunity arises."[7]

In late April, Stuart wrote in his journal that "about an hour before sundown, and while resting from the day's labor, we were startled by several gunshots fired in a clump of cottonwoods. Soon thereafter thirty Indians vociferating 'How-dye-do' and 'Up-sar-O-ka,' which we later found meant Crow Indian in their language [came riding into camp]. I was invited to their camp. While I exchanged lies with them, some of the braves began disputing who would have our best horses. There was thievery all night. At daylight, I aroused the men. As we packed up, the Indians proceeded to forcibly trade for anything they wished. I saw that the time had come to do or die. With one hand full of cartridges and my [Sharps] rifle in the other, I told them to mount their horses and leave camp. They weakened and did."[8]

Twelve years later, when Hauser edited Stuart's journal for publication, he noted that this short comment did not do justice to the tense moment. Stuart, outwardly unperturbed and smoking his pipe, watched until the principal chief was separated from his warriors. Then with a sharp order to his men,

Plate 1. Bozeman, Montana, ca. 1875. The shop of Walter Cooper, Sharps' biggest dealer in Montana, was located below the large rifle on the left. Reproduced from Ralph Heinz, "Montana Sharps," *Man at Arms*, November/December, 1981. Used by permission.

Plate 2. Walter Cooper. Reproduced from Joaquin Miller, *The State of Montana* (Chicago: Houton, Mifflin Co., 1894). Used by permission.

Stuart covered the chief's heart. Each man covered an Indian and every Indian dropped his robe and levelled his gun also. With his eyes flashing, Stuart cursed the old chief for his bad faith and threatened to kill him if he did not call his men off at once. The chief stared at him defiantly for a few seconds. Then Hauser noted, "finally a wave of his hand relieved our doubts and his braves lowered their weapons of death and suddenly sought their robes and ponies."[9]

Hauser laughed and threw his hat in the air. At this he wrote: "The second chief, who was a straight, tall, fine-looking warrior, and as brave as Julius Caeser, was perfectly pale with rage, because the old chief had not signaled the fight, and the fact that I had laughed and exulted over it only increased his rage. Rushing up to me in a white heat, he placed his finger on my nose and then on his own, and quickly touched his gun and then mine, and pointed to one side . . . The young brave had to retire without satisfaction, which I regret to say, he got afterwards."[10]

Several nights later, there were signs that Indians were nearby. Stuart took the first watch and was lying on the ground trying to see what was bothering the horses, when the Indians fired a volley into the camp, killing four horses, woulding two men mortally, another two badly and three slightly.[11]

Hauser was slightly wounded by a ball that was stopped by a memorandum book in his pocket.[12] The Indians fired arrows into the camp all night long. In the morning, a decision was made to abandon all but the necessities and try to escape. The Indians apparently figured Stuart's party had the better "medicine," because they did not attack again. However, another man was lost when he shot himself accidentally. By the time the party returned, it had covered 1,600 miles. James Stuart had used his "trusty" Sharps not only to defend life and property, but also had killed deer, elk, buffalo, and antelope for food along the way.[13]

Sharps rifles were becoming known for their range and accuracy. In May of 1868, the Sioux raided across the Missouri River from Fort Benton. The Indians snatched 15 horses and mules along with 40 head of cattle. While this was going on, the locals raged impotently "for the lack of long range Sharps rifles."[14]

In 1874, 140 men left Bozeman, Montana to open up the Yellowstone River country to settlement and mining. Among the organizers was Bozeman merchant and Sharps dealer Walter Cooper. As the party progressed, they experienced increasing pressure from the Sioux, until at least 600 warriors surrounded them, with more arriving daily. Feeling that the Indians would eventually overpower them, they decided to retreat.

Attacks had been almost constant, when two warriors came out on a hill and fired into camp from a long distance. Jack Beam took a rest and, with careful aim, returned the compliment. Several of the party were looking at the Indians with fieldglasses and declared the ball had hit one. "The distance must have been nearly a mile."[15] Jack used a long-ranged rifle (a 120-grain Sharps) and had made several effective shots on the trip.[16] No tale of the Sharps rifle would be complete without a mile-long shot.

INDIAN FIGHTING

Immediately after the Civil War, the Army sought to secure safe passage to Montana along Bozeman Trail. Near Christmas of 1866, the Army suffered the Fetterman Massacre near Fort Phil Kearney while trying to defend the Bozeman Trail with muzzle-loaders and a few Spencers. Earlier that summer, Montana businessman Nelson Story had made the first cattle drive to Montana with 26 Texans armed with Remington-Geiger breech-loading carbines.

Having been ordered by the Army not to proceed beyond Fort Phil Kearney, the cowboys voted whether to defy the Army's order. All but George Dow voted to proceed. Dow was promptly tied up and tossed into a wagon. He was released 10 miles up the trail, with no option but to continue with the herd. Despite several fights with the Sioux and Cheyenne, the herd successfully reached Montana. The Indians appeared to have more respect for the cowboys and their Remingtons than for the Army.[17] Dow and Story would later be involved in the sale of Sharps rifles at Bozeman.

By late 1866, Fort C.F. Smith on the Montana segment of the Bozeman Trail was down to 10 rounds per man for their Springfield muzzle-loaders.[18] This was not unique to the Army. At the Fetterman Massacre, Crazy Horse carried a Sharps carbine for which he had only four rounds.[19] In late July of 1867, Fort C.F. Smith was finally reinforced. The reinforcements brought with them several hundred .50/70 Model 1866 Springfield rifles, with plenty of ammunition.[20] This was to prove a disastrous surprise to the same Indians who had killed Fetterman and his 80 men just seven months before.[21]

On August 1, 1867, the scene was set. Nine civilians were cutting hay near the fort, with an escort of 20 soldiers who passed the time playing cards and tossing horse shoes. Around 8 am, they were interrupted by an attack from nearly 800 Sioux and Cheyenne warriors. The soldiers retreated into an improvised fort and managed to stand off the Indians all day. Relief finally arrived near night fall. Although three men were killed, the rest survived. Indian casualties had been heavy. After this defeat at the "Hayfield Fight" and a similar one the next day at the "Wagon Box Fight" near Fort Phil Kearney, the Indians would never again launch a full scale attack along the Bozeman Trail.[22] The Army found itself too thinly spread, though, and eventually abandoned the Bozeman Trail forts, once safer ways to Montana had been found.

In these battles and others that followed, the Army made comparatively little use of the Sharps. Even the Seventh Cavalry, however, was issued some converted .50/70 Sharps carbines, prior to their receiving .45/70 Springfield Model 1873 carbines. At the Battle of Allen Creek, Montana on August 11, 1873, the Seventh was mostly armed with the Sharps. Other guns carried in the battle included the Ward-Burton and .50/70 Model 1870 Springfield carbines. With these weapons, they fought a pitched battle with Sioux Indians.[23]

In 1867, the Army set out to pressure the Sioux and Cheyenne who were not on reservations. The Indians joined together in unprecedented numbers and in June were able to defeat General Crook at the Battle of the Rosebud and Custer at the Battle of the Little Big Horn. In both battles, Sharps rifles and carbines were used by both sides. One terrain feature at the Rosebud site is known as Packer's Rocks, where the civilian packers fought using Sharps.[24]

At the Battle of the Little Big Horn, First Sergeant John Ryan used a 15-pound Sharps rifle with a telescopic sight. He had bought the rifle in Bismark, Dakota Territory for $100. Toward the end of the battle, Captain French asked Sergeant Ryan if he could do anything about several Indians shooting beyond the range of the Springfield carbines. Sergeant Ryan fired a couple of shots to get the range, then fired several more shots for effect. These were the last shots of the battle, as the Indian began to pull out. The siege was over.[25]

In 1984 and 1985, extensive archaelogical work was done at the Little Big Horn Battlefield. Many cartridge cases were found. Using modern firearm identification procedures, it was possible to identify 371 individual weapons, 35 of which proved to have been Sharps. While most were probably Indian guns, some were also fired by soldiers and civilians. It is interesting to note that no .44 caliber Sharps bullets or cartridge cases were found.[26] While .44/77 and .44/90 rifles were sold in Montana, they were probably not as popular as rifles using government ammunition.

There are records of several surrenders by the Indians of their arms. In March 1879, Little Wolf's band of Northern Cheyenne surrendered to the Second Cavalry in south-eastern Montana. They turned in 30 firearms.

> 4-Springfield carbines, caliber .45
> 3-Springfield rifles, caliber .50
> 4-Sharps rifles, caliber .45
> 1-Sharps rifle, caliber .50
> 1 Muzzle-loader
> 3-Winchesters or Henrys
> 10 Handguns[27]

No doubt many of the arms surrendered were often unserviceable by Army standards. Also, better arms were probably often appropriated by the soldiers or hidden by the Indians. When Rain-in-the-Face surrendered at Fort Koegh, Montana, he carried a battered .52 caliber Sharps carbine.[28]

SHIPMENTS OF SHARPS RIFLES TO MONTANA

During the period between 1870 and the early 1880s, Sharps rifles were produced by the Sharps Rifle Manufacturing Company of Hartford,

Connecticut and the Sharps Rifle Company of Bridgeport, Connecticut. For our purposes, the two companies can be considered one, since there was continuity between the two firms, and no effect in Montana.

Fortunately the bulk of the records for this period have survived; they are owned by Dr. R.L. Moore, Jr. The records are most complete with regards to the Model 1874, which saw the greatest use in Montana. The data was provided through the very kind assistance of Dr. Moore and was drawn by him directly from the original factory records.

Table A

MONTANA SHIPMENTS OF MODEL 1874 SHARPS RIFLES
FROM FACTORY RECORDS (Approximate)[29]

I.C. Baker Co., Fort Benton	1 -	Sporting Rifle
Adolph Birkenfield, Helena	15 -	Business Rifles
	13 -	Sporting Rifles
Borup & Co. (ordered by Captain John Mix, USA), Fort Custer	20 -	Business Rifles
	1 -	Hunters Rifle
Broadwater, Hubbell, & Co. (ordered by Capt. Mix), Miles City	10 -	Business Rifles
Wm. Coleman & Co., Butte	10 -	Business Rifles
Wm. Coleman & Co., Deer Lodge	10 -	Business Rifles
N. Connelly, Phillipsburg	4 -	Business Rifles
Walter Cooper, Bozeman	5 -	Carbines*
	141 -	Military Rifles**
	55 -	Sporting Rifles
J.G. Dow (most, possibly all went to Cooper), Bozeman	100 -	Business Rifles
	35 -	Carbines
	3 -	Long Range #1
	5 -	Mid Range #1
	60 -	Sporting Rifles
S.T. Hauser (also possibly in the Rifles records as Hansen or Hanson)***	3 -	Creedmoor Rifles
John Houck (also possibly spelled Houk), Pioneer City	1 -	Sporting Rifle
George Laughlin, Helena	2 -	Sporting Rifles
J.L. Pemberton, Deer Lodge	2 -	Sporting Rifles
Granville Stuart (also possibly in the records as Stewart)	5 -	Sporting Rifles
B.H. Tatem (also possibly in the records as Tatum)	1 -	Sporting Rifle
C.O. Trask, Bannock	15 -	Sporting Rifles
TOTAL SHIPPED TO MONTANA BY SHARPS FACTORY	517 -	Rifles and Carbines

*These five Carbines are probably Model 1869s. They are outside the normal serial number range of either the Model 1869 or Model 1874, being five digit serial numbers. This would place them within the serial number range assigned to percussion guns. Several other Model 1869s, however, are known with similar serial numbers. Normal serial number range of the Model 1869 would be around 150,000 (Or CL00), with the Model 1874 following.

**Twenty-five of these Military Rifles are shown in the Company records as being "Rimfire."

***There are several names with one or more alternative spellings. The most obvious reason for this was the difficulty in reading what a person wrote. In the case of S.T. Hauser, his signature sometimes looked like "Hansen." In the case of Granville Stuart, "Stewart" would be the more common of the two. Even in a three-volume history of Montana published shortly after his death, his name is spelled "Stewart." I have tried to show the preferred form first, with alternatives after.

Dr. Moore classified this information as approximate. Some serial numbers do not appear in the factory records. However, this is the most accurate number possible. It can be considered as essentially correct.

<u>Table B</u>

NUMBER OF MODEL 1874 SHARPS RIFLES SHIPPED
TO MONTANA BY PURCHASER

		TOTAL
I.G. Baker Co.	1 - Sporting Rifle	1
Adolph Birenfield	15 - Business Rifles	
	13 - Sporting Rifles	
		28
Borup & Co. (ordered by	20 - Business Rifles	
Captain Mix)	1 - Hunters Rifle	
		21
Broadwater, Hubbell & Co.	10 - Rifles	10
(ordered by Capt. Mix)		
Wm. Coleman & Co.	20 - Business Rifles	20
N. Connelly	4 - Business Rifles	4
Walter Cooper	5 - Carbines	
	141 - Military Rifles	
	55 - Sporting Rifles	
		201
J.G. Dow (most to Cooper)	100 - Business Rifles	
	35 - Carbines	
	3 - Long Range #1	
	5 - Mid Range #1	
	60 - Sporting Rifles	
		203
S.T. Hauser	3 - Creedmoor Rifles	3
John Houck	1 - Sporting Rifle	1
George Laughlin	2 - Sporting Rifles	2
J.L. Pemberton	2 - Sporting Rifles	2
Granville Stuart	5 - Sporting Rifles	4
B.H. Tatem	1 - Sporting Rifles	1
C.O. Trask	15 - Sporting Rifles	15

TOTAL RIFLES SHIPPED TO MONTANA
FROM THE FACTORY   517

Table C

NUMBER OF MODEL 1874 SHARPS SHIPPED FROM
THE FACTORY TO MONTANA, BY PLACE

		TOTAL
Bannock		
C.O. Trask	15 - Sporting Rifles	15
Bozeman		
Walter Cooper	5 - Carbines	
	141 - Military Rifles	
	55 - Sporting Rifles	
	201	
J.G. Dow (most to Cooper)	100 - Business Rifles	
	35 - Carbines	
	3 - Long Range #1	
	5 - Mid Range #1	
	60 - Sporting Rifles	
	203	404
Butte		
Wm. Coleman & Co.	10 - Business Rifles	10
Deer Lodge		
Wm. Coleman & Co.	10 - Business Rifles	
J.L. Pemberton	2 - Sporting Rifles	
Granville Stuart	4 - Sporting Rifles	
	17	17
Fort Benton		
I.G. Baker & Co.	1 - Sporting Rifle	1
Fort Custer		
Borup & Co. (Capt. Mix)	20 - Business Rifles	
	1 - Hunters Rifle	
	21	21
Helena		
Adolph Birkenfield	15 - Business Rifles	
	13 - Sporting Rifles	
	28	
S.T. Hauser	3 - Creedmoor	
George Laughlin	2 - Sporting Rifles	
B.T. Tatem	1 - Sporting Rifle	
	34	34
Miles City		
Broadwater, Hubbell & Co. (Capt. Mix)	10 - Business Rifles	10
Phillipsburg		
N. Connelly	4 - Business Rifles	4
Pioneer City		
John Houck	1 - Sporting Rifle	1
TOTAL SHIPPED TO MONTANA		517

Table D

NUMBER OF MODEL 1874 SHARPS RIFLES SHIPPED
BY THE FACTORY TO MONTANA, BY TYPE

	TOTAL
Business Rifles*	169
Carbines, Model 1869	5
Carbines, Model 1874	35
Creedmoor Rifles	3
Hunters Rifle	1
Long Range #1	3
Mid Range #1	5
Military Rifles (Centerfire)*	116
Military Rifles (Rimfire)*	25
Sporting Rifles	155
TOTAL SHIPPED TO MONTANA, BY TYPE	517

*The numbers of Business Rifles and Military Rifles shipped approach 10 percent of the numbers of these models manufactured. In addition the "Rimfire" Military Rifles are virtually unique. There were no recorded sales of Express Rifles, Schuetzen Rifle, or "A" Model rifles to Montana.

Captain John Mix, USA apparently had almost a dealer status; he ordered a number of rifles to be shipped to several dealers in the territory.[30] "The Department of the Dakotas" was an Army designation which included Montana, as well as North and South Dakota.[31]

The most popular type of rifle shipped by the factory to Montana was the Business Rifle, with 169 rifles shipped. Next came the Sporting Rifles, with 155 rifles shipped. A close third were Military Rifles, with 141 rifles shipped. I suspect that some of the Military Rifles shipped to Cooper and other Western dealers were stripped of their barrels and forearms, then equipped with double set triggers, a new barrel and forearm and sold as Sporting Rifles. Military Rifles were significantly cheaper than Sporting Rifles.

Do the figures given for factory shipments to Montana represent all the new Sharps rifles sent to Montana? Unfortunately not. Walter Cooper, for instance, bought significant quantities of rifles from B. Kittredge & Co. Recently records for the sales of Sharps rifles by Schuyler, Hartley, & Graham have been donated to the Buffalo Bill Historical Center. Perhaps these might hold some answers, although the records I have seen did not seem to show any shipments to Montana. Still it is quite likely that a significant number of Sharps were shipped to Montana from sources other than the factory.

Considering that less than 13,000 of the Model 1874 Sharps were produced, and that Montana had a population of only 20,000 in 1868 and 40,000 in 1880, it is apparent that the Sharps was very popular in Montana.

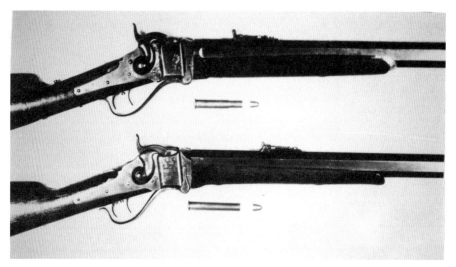

Plate 3. Two Sharps rifles from Walter Cooper's shop. The top rifle is a .40/90 Sharps BN, with a Hartford-style forearm cap; it weighed 16 pounds. The bottom rifle is a .45-2 7/8 inch Sharps, with a Bridgeport-style forearm; it weighs 14-1/2 pounds. Reproduced from Ralph Heinz, "Montana Sharps," *Man at Arms*, November/December, 1981. Used by permission.

WALTER COOPER
From W. Cooper, Esq., Bozeman, Montana, April 9, 1872:

> Those four guns you sent me take the eye of every one. They out-
> shoot anything ever brought to this country. I won a bet of ten dol-
> lars the other day on penetration against an army musket,—called
> the Springfield Needle Gun here. Shot the same powder and shot
> two inches deeper into the woods.[32]

This recommendation from Walter Cooper was printed in the *1875 Sharps
Manufacturing Catalog*. Cooper was far and away the largest dealer for
Sharps in Montana. Unfortunately, the arrangement between Cooper and
Sharps was not always profitable. Cooper was born on July 4, 1843 in Sterling,
New York. In his later years, he left some autobiographical notes, now at
Montana State University, Bozeman, Montana. In them, he noted: "Having
established a business and home in the city of Bozeman the last of December
1868. Handling as specialties: Firearms, ammunition, and a general line of
hunting and defensive material together with a first class gunsmith establish-
ment so useful and necessary in this far off country. New and growing, having
little or nothing, demanding everything . . . Home of a large number of Indian
tribes many of whom roamed at large."

By the early part of 1873, the gun business had not grown as Cooper had
expected. By November 6, 1876, Edwin G. Wescott, president of the Sharps
Rifle Co. noted that some bills were as much as four years old. This continued
until orders were being handled through J.G. Dow, cashier of the First
National Bank. A September 28, 1878 letter noted that the B. Kittredge
Company had taken up Cooper's note for $1,800. On October 15, 1878,
Sharps wrote that 60 Sporting Rifles had been sent on consignment. In a letter
on January 15, 1879, however, Sharps noted with regret that Cooper had to
close and wishes his successors well. It is interesting that although this matter
had gone on some time, the relationship was still friendly.[33]

Succeeding Cooper was the firm of Story and Goewey. Their first ad in
Bozeman's *Avant Courier* appeared on December 19, 1878. The last appeared
on March 3, 1881. Apparently, Cooper took the business back, as new ads for
Cooper's Armory appeared on April 28, 1881 (see Plate 4). They last appeared
on December 18, 1884. These ads carried the notice that "Persons indebted to
the late firm of Story & Goewey will save trouble by calling at once and mak-
ing an early settlement."[34]

Walter Cooper had better luck in his other business ventures. He helped to
found the towns of Red Lodge, Laurel, and Bridger. He helped supply
Bozeman with its first water system. Also he was involved with one of the
largest flour mills in the territory and with varied mining enterprises.[35]

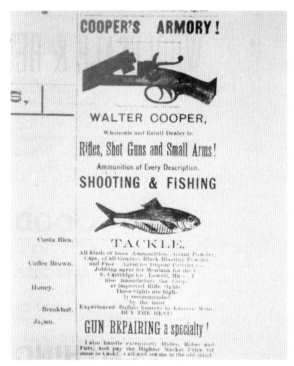

Plate 4. An advertisement for Walter Cooper which appeared in the *Avant Courier*. Reproduced from Ralph Heinz, "Montana Sharps," *Man at Arms*, November/December, 1981. Used by permission.

Besides selling rifles, Walter Cooper had an extensive gunsmithing business, which produced some interesting weapons bearing the stamp of Walter Cooper-Bozeman, M.T. (see Plate 5).

Visually, his sights and pewter forend caps stand out the most. While several Cooper sights are known, he is perhaps best known for his rear sight, which offered the convenience of a large easy-to-see buckhorn sight and the standard flip-up Lawrence sight leaf for long-range shooting (see Plates 6 and 7). The rear sight was fitted with a white platinum line next to the eye, which helped the eye catch the sight in the bright western sun. With a later "improved" rear sight, the buckhorn could be raised to give two quick sight positions.[36]

Walter Cooper's front sights were some of the earliest to combine the use of ivory, or in some cases gold, platinum or phosphor bronze, in a sight sturdy enough to stand frontier usage. Cooper claimed that under some light conditions, only his sights could be seen clearly. On November 14, 1882, Walter Cooper was granted his only sight patent, No. 267,497, for the Cooper Open Front Sight with gauge. This sight had projections or "pin-balls" approximately

Plate 5. Walter Cooper's stamp. Reproduced from Ralph Heinz, "Montana Sharps," *Man at Arms,* November/December, 1981. Used by permission.

halfway up the sight, which in effect gave the front sight two different range settings without adjusting the rear sight (see Plate 8).[37]

Plate 6. A Walter Cooper rear sight. This view shows the use of a normal Lawrence rear sight, with a new rear sight dovetailed into the slot that replaces the part of the Lawrence sight that keeps it centered. Courtesy Gerald R. Mayberry.

Plate 7. A side view of the sight described in Plate 6. Courtesy Gerald R. Mayberry.

Most Sharps rifles made at Hartford had forend caps of pewter. Later when the company moved to Bridgeport, this was largely dropped. Some Western dealers, however, continued to order this feature. Walter Cooper had his own

Plate 8. Walter Cooper's style of forearm cap was unique to his shop. Reproduced from Ralph Heinz, "Montana Sharps," *Man at Arms*, November/December, 1981. Used by permission.

version, which is more squared off than the Sharps style. Many rifles that his shop worked on have this feature (see Plate 9).[38]

Plate 9. A Walter Cooper front sight. Faintly visible is the ivory insert in the blade and the three small pins that hold it in place. Courtesy Gerald R. Mayberry.

Other modifications were made to Sharps rifles by Cooper's shop. A rebounding hammer was sometimes added to return the hammer to half cock when it is fired. On a few rifles that Cooper worked on, the top edge of the breechblock, or slide, as it was called by Sharps, has been ground to provide a beveled surface to cam a hard-to-chamber cartridge into the chamber. This perhaps lessens the protection from a blown primer, but it would probably result in difficult extraction of the fired case.[39] Freund's true camming breechblock, with two extractors, really was a better idea, although significantly more expensive.

Because his shop was a full service gunsmith shop, many rifles with Cooper's stamp have been rebarreled and/or restocked. The frontier was hard on all stocks, not just Sharps. Barrels were made of relatively soft metal, which could be shot out through heavy use. Also, a customer might wish a new or special caliber. E.C. Meacham's conversions of Civil War percussion guns were often rebarreled to overcome the objections of hunters, who felt the barrels used were cheap and inferior. As Ralph Heinz has noted, Walter Cooper guns are probably the most Montana of all Montana Sharps.[40]

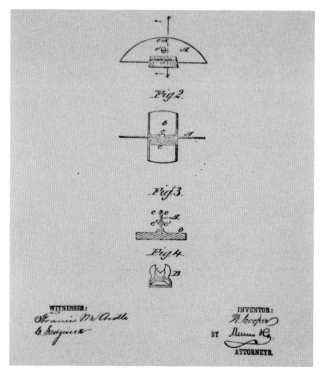

Plate 10. A copy of the patent drawing for a Cooper front sight of different design. Courtesy Ralph Heinz.

ALEXANDER D. MCAUSLAND

Three hundred miles east of Bozeman lies Miles City. Shortly after the Battle of the Little Big Horn, Fort Keogh was built on the banks of the Yellowstone River. Miles Town, later Miles City, grew up fast around the fort, in the heart of the northern range of the buffalo. Other game was present in vast numbers as well. Later, after the buffalo were gone, this area would become one of America's greatest cattle ranges.

One dealer and gunsmith was located in Miles City, Alexander D. McAusland. While the records of the Sharps Rifle Company fail to show that any Sharps were shipped to him there, there are records of Sharps being shipped to him at Omaha. Probably he obtained his Sharps from dealers such as B. Kittredge & Company.

Alexander D. McAusland was born in Dunbarton, Scotland in 1835.[41] His parents emigrated to the United States, bringing the family with them. His father, A.D. McAusland, Sr., was also a gun store proprietor. About 1875, McAusland followed the rush to the Black Hills. Apparently he didn't find the success he sought. Looking for better opportunities, McAusland left

Deadwood for Miles City. Walking through very cold weather, he arrived in Miles City on Christmas Eve 1879. He went to the only place open, a saloon, where, as he was unloading his Sharps, it discharged into the dirt floor, creating a cloud of dust and smoke.[42]

McAusland opened a business which he called the Creedmore Armory. He is remembered partly because a number of rebarrelled Sharps rifles bear his stamp (see Plate 11). A 26-pound rifle with his stamp, heavy even by Sharps standards, is known. Elmer Keith wrote that any Sharps over 16 pounds tended to rotate the saddle if carried in a scabbard.

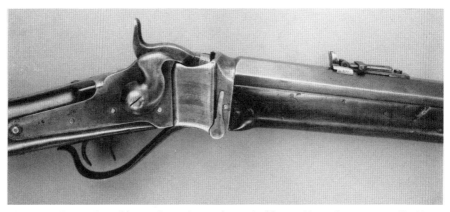

Plate 11. Rifle Number 144,978. Shipped as a 14-pound, .44/90 to T.E. Jackson, Fort Griffin, Texas on July 1, 1876. Rebarrelled to .45-2 7/8 inch, 15-pound by A.D. McAusland of Miles City, Montana. A true buffalo gun, it also has Cooper sights. Courtesy Gerald R. Mayberry.

As Miles City was at the heart of the buffalo trade in the early 1880s, business must have been very good for a time. A.D. McAusland stayed active in the business until 1918, when at the age of 83 he sold the business to his longtime friend and associate, W.H. Crouse. Crouse was a violin maker and violinist, who also made rifle stocks for McAusland. A.D. McAusland returned to Omaha, where he died the next year. Crouse kept the shop open until 1950.[43]

Though the Sharps Rifle Company records show no rifles shipped to A.D. McAusland in Miles City, they do show a few Business Rifles shipped to Broadwater, Hubbel & Co. The *Yellowstone Journal* also mentions or carries ads for J. Basinski General Merchandise, W.A. Burleigh General Merchandise, Savage's Store as dealers in arms and ammunition. John Rohner also advertised both gunsmithing and sewing machine repair.[44]

THE HUNTING SHARPS

While Indian fighting suggests more romance than it perhaps deserves, the fact remains that for every shot fired in anger, many times that were fired in hunting. The sheer size of the Montana territory—100,000,000 acres—made hunting a necessity. Even at restaurants and grocery stores, much of the meat available was often supplied by market hunters. The *Yellowstone Journal* of January 17, 1880 showed buffalo meat selling at two to three cents per pound.

One to whom a Sharps was shipped was John K. Houck of Pioneer City, Montana (see Plate 12). Houck came to Montana in 1862, having failed to find his fortune in California. As was often the case on the frontier, he had a variety of jobs and businesses, working as a store keeper, packer, supplier of charcoal to the mines, and as a prospector and miner.[45] The rifle Houck ordered from Sharps is a .40/70 Sporting Rifle that survives today. The factory records show that it was shipped to Pioneer City, Montana during July, 1878.[46]

This rifle was probably used on an occasion when Houck was sleeping near his corral. In the corral were a cow and her calf; outside it were a couple of interested parties. Houck was awakened by the noise of a bear attacking the calf. Planting the muzzle of his gun upon the bear's head, he fired and old "Bruin" fell dead. Ten minutes later, another bear attacked the calf and was also shot. In the morning, Houck found one dead bear in the corral and the other nearby. Apparently the long-range of the Sharps' accuracy was not needed that night.[47]

Plate 12. Main Street, Pioneer City, Montana. A Sharps rifle was shipped to John Houk (also spelled "Houck") while he lived here. Courtesy Gary Roedl.

Another hunter using a Sharps was Andrew Garcia, who bought his rifle from Walter Cooper. When he died in 1943, he left a manuscript of his experiences. *A Tough Trip Through Paradise* records enough adventure for several lifetimes.

In 1878 Walter Cooper trusted Garcia with $300 worth of goods. He already had a Model 1873 Winchester carbine. "But [I] had to buy a buffalo gun. Like the Chinaman who took the largest sized boot if it was the same price as the smaller to get more leather for the money, I bought a .45/120 caliber Sharps rifle, buffalo gun which weighed 15 pounds and cost $75. Although I could have had a lighter .45/90 #13 for the same price." He was probably happy to have spent the money one dark night, when he had to kill at short range a large grizzly that attacked him and his wife in camp.[48]

Early Montana was a hunter's paradise. While most hunting was to supply the frontiersman's needs, the sport hunter came early as well. By the last part of the 19th century, not just the buffalo, but much of the other large game had been severely reduced in numbers.

Dr. George Bird Grinnel (1849-1938) is best known for his writings on the Plains Indians. He also was editor of *Forest and Stream* from 1876 till 1911 and was the driving force behind the foundling of Glacier National Park. James Willard Schultz later noted that in 1883, "During our hunt, Dr. Grinnel killed a large ram at long-range, offhand, with one shot from his old Sharps rifle . . . I therefore named the site Single-Shot Mountain."[49] Nearby Gunsight Mountain and Lake in Glacier National Park probably were also named on this trip.[50]

George Shields also hunted on more than one occasion in Montana. His guide was often Miles City photographer L.A. Huffman (see Plate 13). On one occasion, Huffman emptied his Kennedy .44/40's magazine and all the cartridges in his belt into a herd of elk at ranges under 75 yards. Several were wounded, but none killed. This shows why a rifle of the Sharps power was necessary for hunting large game.[51]

Shields used a .40/75 Model 1878 Sharps, sometimes at least with explosive bullets, which he felt gave satisfactory service. A strong supporter of Sharps rifles, he once wrote: "A large majority of the frontiersmen I met . . . used Sharps rifles . . . as to their effectiveness and adaptation to frontier use, they pronounced them the best arm in use."[52]

W.O. Pickett wrote the following testimonial to Sharps. It appeared in their last two catalogs.

> To Sharps Rifle Co.
> St. Louis, MO., December 15, 1877
>
> Dear sirs-I have just returned from a trip to Montana, where the past eighteen months have been spent hunting large game in that magnificent game country. During that time, I have used exclusively the Long-Range Sharps, .44 calibre, bought of you in June 1876, and take pleasure in testifying to the satisfaction it has given. I traveled

2,200 miles with it slung to the horn of my saddle, discharged it 2,500 times, was exposed to numerous snow and rain storms, was "bucked off" several times by a "Cayuse" horse, yet it was never once out of order, nor did it fail to do its duty when held right and with properly loaded shells. I hunted all types of game, with which that country abounds, and killed antelope, white and black tail deer, elk, buffalo, grizzly bear, yet the rifling is as bright, and the gun is substantially as good as when I bought it. Were I to go on such a trip again, I would select the same class of gun instead of the "sporting guns" usually taken. I was glad I selected the "straight" stock instead of the pistol "grip" as the letter would not have taken the usage received. . . [53]

UNITED IN DEATH.

Plate 13. G.O. Shields with a bear and an elk. This image was made from an L.A. Huffman photograph. Reproduced from G.O. Shields, *Rustling in the Rockies* (Chicago: Belford, Clarke & Co., 1883). Used by permission.

BUFFALO HUNTING

The single most important use of the Sharps rifle in Montana was in another type of hunting. Asked how many buffalo there were, an Indian answered, "The country is as one robe."[54] In other words, it was covered by buffalo. By 1884, the buffalo were gone.

During a four-month hunt, Sam McGuire and three other men marketed 3,800 buffalo hides, 4,000 buffalo tongues, and 1,800 antelope. The camp outfit consisted of 50-pound sack of flour, 50 pounds of sugar, 50 pounds of coffee, a side of bacon, beans, baking powder, and 50 pounds of dried fruit. The most essential item was ammunition, consisting of 100 to 500 pounds of lead, 50 to 100 pounds of powder, primer, paper, and 500 cartridge cases. The weapons used were the .45/120 and .40/90 Sharps.[55]

A correspondent from *Forest and Stream* noted "that sharp wicked crack I knew came from Price's .40/90. No other gun talks like a .40 caliber Sharps with 90 grains of Dupont."[56]

Other buffalo hunters of the period were Vic Smith, "Doc" Zahl, John Cook, "Hi" Bickerdyke, John Goff and Steele Frazier. Most of the vast buffalo range lay between the Yellowstone and Missouri Rivers. Hides went for between $1.25 and $3.50 each.[57]

Mark Brown wrote: "Theodore Roosevelt, who saw [the buffalo hunters] after the herds were gone, noted that they 'formed a distinct class' and were absolutely shiftless and improvident; . . . had no settled habits; . . . were inured to steady work; . . . and that many drifted into criminal occupations." On the range they were rough looking individuals—usually dirty, greasy, unshaven, and frequently lousy—but usually hospitable and ready to help in time of need. John Goff, who had hunted in Texas before Montana, was once described by a buffalo hunter, who was probably dirty and unkempt himself, as having "long hair and was the dirtiest, greasiest and smokiest looking mortal I had ever seen, as he sat there on a fleet-looking horse, holding in his hands a .44 Sharps' rather carelessly . . . After we reached his camp, he treated me like a nobleman."[58]

In Miles City, some buffalo hunters would enter a bar and reach inside their clothes to see who could catch the first louse for drinks.[59]

Montana did have game laws. From 1878, it was unlawful to take buffalo, elk, deer, mountain sheep, goat or antelope between the first of February and the tenth of August. It was also unlawful to kill animals for their hides alone,[60] a provision that appears to have been little enforced. The extermination of the buffalo came later in Montana than further south. The best hunting years were in the early 1880s.

Probably the most successful buffalo hunter of all time was Jim White. White came north from Texas, when that hunt was over. In 1878, he met Oliver Perry Hanna, who would later write his memoirs of the buffalo range. Having joined together to fill a meat contract with the Army, they came on some deer at a range of 400 or 500 yards. White said, "[W]e better take a shot at them before we go back to camp." Hanna began to think of how to get closer, when White got out a 16-pound Sharps rifle. White's first shot was under the belly of one. The second killed one. Soon there were nine deer down. Hanna told White "that he had never seen shooting like that." White told Hanna "to take one of the three 16 pound rifles and practice at long range." Soon Hanna was able to kill at long range too.[61]

The trajectory of these old guns is every bit as curved as was always thought. The buffalo hunters developed the skill of estimating range and combined that with a real knowledge of the ability of their Sharps. Those skills made them some of the best shots America ever produced.

By the time of the buffalo hunt in Montana, buffalo hunting had been refined to a science. Hanna noted that

> we would get a stand on them . . . they travel in large droves . . . When we got within range, we would both begin shooting rapidly, always shooting the leaders. When we had shot the leaders, the drove would stop . . . Then we would wound two or three, they would walk around among the others, smelling of blood, which would cause the others to mill around. From that time on only one man would shoot, while the other cooled the guns with water, cleaned and reloaded them, taking turns at shooting. Every little while one buffalo would start to take the lead and we would get him. Sometimes we would get forty or fifty, all the men could skin in one day.

Jim White was credited with 19,000 buffalo between 1872 and 1880. White did not live to see the end of the buffalo; he was murdered in 1880.[62]

In 1882, the Northern Pacific Railroad alone shipped 200,000 hides. Many others went by steamboat, as many as 10,000 per trip. In 1884, the railroad carried 100 hides. A single pile of 600 tons of bones testified to the size of the kill. The pile could be seen from 40 miles away, glistening in the sun.[63]

The final extermination of the buffalo insured that the Indian would forever be dependent on the reservation. Their way of life was gone. Even on the reservations, supplies could be inadequate. During the winter of 1883-84, nearly 600 Blackfeet starved to death.[64]

The day of the Sharps passed with the buffalo and thousands of other large game animals. The guns had perhaps outlived the company that made them, and a few exist today. But many others didn't survive. Several Sharps hung above L.A. Huffman's fireplace in Miles City (see Plate 14). Also built into the fireplace are several Sharps rifle barrels. It is thought that the actions are also built into the wall. A time came when a Sharps was worth nothing more than a "hook." Battered and rusty they may be, but treasure those that have survived. When you look at them, you are looking at history.

Plate 14. L.A. Huffman's fireplace, with three Sharps rifles hanging above it and two Sharps rifle barrels projecting from its face. Courtesy Bill Felton.

NOTES

1. Louis A. Garavaglia and Charles Worman, *Firearms of the American West: 1803-65* (Albuquerque: University of New Mexico Press, 1984), p. 242.
2. Garavaglia and Worman, *Firearms of the American West: 1803-65*, p. 243.
3. Garavaglia and Worman, *Firearms of the American West: 1803-65*, p. 246.
4. *History of Montana* (Chicago: Warner, Beers & Co., 1885), pp. 60-74.
5. *History of Montana*, pp. 60-74.
6. *History of Montana*, pp. 60-74.
7. *History of Montana*, pp. 60-74.
8. *History of Montana*, pp. 60-74.
9. Mark H. Brown, *The Plainsmen of the Yellowstone* (New York: C.P. Putnam's Sons, 1961), pp. 130-133.
10. Brown, *The Plainsmen of the Yellowstone*, pp. 130-133.
11. *History of Montana*, pp. 60-74.
12. Brown, *The Plainsmen of the Yellowstone*, pp. 130-133.
13. *History of Montana*, pp. 60-74.
14. Joel Overholser, *Fort Benton* (Fort Benton: Joel Overholser, 1987), p. 314.
15. Overholser, *Fort Benton*, p. 380.
16. *History of Montana*, p. 86.
17. Robert A. Murray, *The Bozeman Trail* (Boulder, Colorado: Pruett Publishing, 1988), p. 37.
18. Brown, *The Plainsmen of the Yellowstone*, p. 173.
19. Wayne R. Austerman, "Speaks Far Gun," *Man at Arms*, March/April 1984, p. 14.
20. Brown, *The Plainsmen of the Yellowstone*, p. 173.
21. Murray, *The Bozeman Trail*, p. 45.
22. Murray, *The Bozeman Trail*, pp. 51-52.
23. Letter from Ralph Heinz, June 8, 1992.
24. Letter from Ralph Heinz, June 29, 1991.
25. Ralph Heinz, *First Sergeant Ryan* (Big Timber: C. Sharps Arms Co., 1982), pp. 1-2.
26. Douglas A. Scott, R.A. Fox, M.A. Connor, and Dick Harmon, *Archaeological Perspective on the Battle of the Little Bighorn* (Norman: University of Oklahoma Press, 1989), pp. 153-182.
27. Louis A. Garavaglia and Charles Worman, *Firearms of the American West: 1866-94* (Albuquerque: University of New Mexico Press, 1985), pp. 369-70.
28. Garavaglia and Worman, *Firearms in the American West: 1866-94*, pp. 369-70.
29. Letter from Dr. R.L. Moore, Jr., September 14, 1992.
30. Letter from Dr. R.L. Moore, Jr., August 11, 1992.
31. Conversation with Ralph Heinz, September 18, 1992.
32. *1875 Sharps Rifle Manufacturing Co. Catalog*, p. 22.
33. Letter from Dr. R.L. Moore, Jr., to Ralph Heinz, July 20, 1980.
34. Avant Courier, Bozeman, Montana, December 18, 1884.
35. Ralph Heinz, "Montana Sharps," *Man at Arms*, November/December 1981, pp. 24-37.
36. Arthur Corbin Gould, *Modern American Rifles* (Boston: Bradley Whidden, 1891).
37. Gould, *Modern American Rifles*.
38. Heinz, "Montana Sharps," pp. 24-37.
39. Heinz, "Montana Sharps," pp. 24-37.
40. Heinz, "Montana Sharps," pp. 24-37.
41. *1860 Nebraska Census*, p. 5. I'd like to thank Gary Roedl for providing this document.
42. Letter from W.R. Felton, Jr., to Gary Roedl, February 15, 1989.
43. Bill Barnhart, "A McAusland Sharps," *Arms Gazette,* August 1979, pp. 38-40.
44. *Yellowstone Journal*, Miles City, various issues from 1880-84.
45. Joaquin Miller, *The State of Montana* (Chicago: Houghton, Mifflin Co., 1894), pp. 695-97.

46. Dr. R.L. Moore, Jr., factory letter, May 1, 1989.
47. Miller, *The State of Montana*, pp. 695-97.
48. Andrew Garcia, *Tough Trip Through Paradise* (Boston: Houghton, Mifflin Co., 1967).
49. Robert Fletcher, *Montana's Historical Markers* (Helena: Montana Historical Society, 1989), p. 12.
50. James Willart Schultz, "Return to the Beloved Mountains," *Montana*, 3-57, p. 21.
51. G.O. Shields, *Rustling in the Rockies* (Chicago: Belford, Clarke & Co., 1883), pp. 26-35.
52. Shields, *Rustling in the Rockies*, pp. 151-52.
53. *1880 Sharps Rifle Co. Catalog*, pp. 37-38.
54. *We Seized Our Rifles*, Lee Silliman, ed. (Missoula: Mountain Press, 1982), p. 137.
55. B.F. Lamb, "The Passing of the Buffalo," in J.K. Howard, *Montana Margins* (New Haven: Yale University Press, 1946), pp. 410-413.
56. Garavaglia and Worman, *Firearms of the American West: 1866-94*, p. 201.
57. Brown, *The Plainsmen of the Yellowstone*, pp. 362-69.
58. Mark Brown, *The Frontier Years* (New York: Bramhall House, 1955), p. 68.
59. Brown, *The Frontier Years*, pp. 241-42.
60. *Yellowstone Journal*, March 13, 1880, front page.
61. Oliver Perry Hanna, "My Life as a Buffalo Hunter," in Miles Gilbert, *Getting a Stand* (Tempe: Miles Gilbert, 1986), pp. 121-163.
62. Hanna, "My Life as a Buffalo Hunter," pp. 121-163.
63. David Walter, "Final Hour," *Montana Magazine*, November/December 1988, pp. 52-58.
64. Helen West, "Starvation Winter of the Blackfeet," *Montana*, Winter 1959, pp. 2-19.

"THE APPEARANCE OF EVIDENCE"
A Brief Examination of the Life and Work of Herman Leslie Ulrich

by Herbert G. Houze

In the study of art, the attribution or identification of unsigned pieces as being from the hand of a particular engraver, painter or sculptor is always problematic. Although some degree of certainty can be achieved if an attribution is based upon comparison with a number of signed or otherwise positively identified pieces, due to the anonymous nature of unsigned works, absolute proof is always lacking. Further affecting this process is, as Jonathan Richardson the Elder noted two and a half centuries ago, the fact that the appearance of evidence is different to each observer.[1] Thus, the ultimate acceptance or rejection of an attribution are matters based not only upon study but also personal belief tempered by emotion.

Within the study of 19th- and early 20th-century American firearms decoration the attribution of unsigned work has in the past not been terribly precise. In part, this was substantially due to the marked lack of any considerable body of signed work to use as a comparison base, as well as the simplistic approaches taken to the subject by the majority of researchers. For the most part, attributions have primarily been based upon the manufacturer of particular arms together with the dates specific engravers worked (or are presumed to have worked) for them, and the resemblance of the decoration to that encountered on like firearms of comparable dates. The former course, however, can result in what Sir John Pope-Hennessy describes as the tendency of some observers "to construct from authenticated works an ideal image of an artist, and to free it of those [works] which seem not to conform."[2] Though rarely mentioned, there is also the corollary to Pope-Hennessy's remark of attributing to the hand of a particular artist those unsigned works which would enhance the desired image that are, in fact, the work of others.

Plate 1: Tintype photograph of Herman L. Ulrich circa 1868. Ulrich Family Papers.

To a great extent, these processes have given rise to the creation of a patheon of arms engravers—Cuno Helfricht, Louis D. Nimschke, Conrad F. Ulrich, John Ulrich and Gustave Young—whose work is known from both signed examples as well as personal and corporate records. The contributions of other engravers, many of whom are unfortunately anonymous, have as a result been dismissed as being of little consequence. More disturbing, though, has been the tendency on the part of some researchers to attribute unsigned work which exhibits any degree of merit exclusively to members of the pantheon.

One engraver whose work has remained unrecognized due to this is Herman Leslie Ulrich (1846-1937). In part, the anonymity of his work has also been the result not only of its misattribution to the hands of his brothers Conrad and John,[3] but also to more than a modest amount of purposeful deception by them.[4] Yet despite these complications, the work executed by H.L. Ulrich between approximately 1870 and 1918 can be identified. As a result, it has therefore been possible to rehabilitate his reputation as an engraver of considerable importance whose talents were sought after by a number of clients.

Herman Leslie Ulrich was born on September 24, 1846, the third son of Conrad and Marguerite Viel Ulrich, in Mansbach, Germany.[5] Shortly after the 1848 Revolution, the Ulrich family emigrated to the United States, arriving in New York in mid-1849, aboard the auxilliary steam-powered sailing vessel The George William. It is evident that the elder Ulrich children had already received some art training by this time, judging from the paper silhouette pictures of game animals they cut to pass the time during the voyage, which have been preserved among the family's papers. Although Conrad Ulrich initially settled in New York City, he subsequently moved to Hartford, Connecticut, in 1852. Family tradition holds that this move was prompted by the fact that Conrad had met Samuel Colt during the latter's European tour of 1849. As the other Ulrich relatives who had emigrated to the United States, both before and after Conrad, settled in the Midwest, some credence should be accorded this tradition. Additional support is provided by the fact that when Conrad Ulrich relocated to Hartford, he immediately entered the employ of the Colt's Patent Fire Arms Manufacturing Company. While absolute proof is lacking, it is believed that Herman Ulrich was apprenticed to one or the other of the Colt company's engraving contractors, Herman Bodenstein or Gustave Young, in about 1860. By 1867, Herman Ulrich had completed his apprenticeship, and in that year's Hartford city directory advertised himself as an engraver.[6] In late July of 1870, he moved from Hartford to New Haven, where he was hired on the 29th by the Winchester Repeating Arms Company to do their engraving work on a contract basis at a salary of 32.5 cents per hour.[7] Over the period of the next five years Ulrich worked for the Winchester company as chief engraver from July 29, 1870 to March 1871; as engraving contractor with his brother Conrad Friedrich Ulrich from April, 1871 to March, 1874; and as chief engraving contractor from May, 1874 to May 29, 1875.[8]

The earliest surviving example of Ulrich's work for the Winchester Repeating Arms Company which can be identified with certainty is a Model 1866 Rifle serial number 26283 (Plates 2 to 4) that was prepared for the company's display at the Exposition of the American Institute held in New

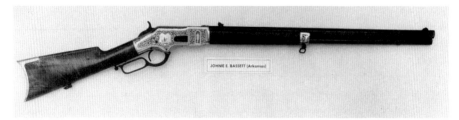

Plate 2: Winchester Model 1866 Rifle, serial number 26283, engraved by H.L.Ulrich in the late summer of 1870 for exhibition by the Winchester Repeating Arms Company at the Exposition of the American Institute in New York City. Formerly in the collection of the late Johnie E. Bassett. Olin Corporation Photograph, Winchester Arms Collection Archives, Cody Firearms Museum, Buffalo Bill Historical Center, Cody, Wyoming.

York in the autumn of 1870, and which has been credited in the past to Gustave Young.[9] The decoration of this rifle, which was formerly in the Johnie E. Bassett Collection, consists of subsidiary scroll engraving on the muzzle and breech of the barrel as well as the forend cap and buttplate tang. (The photographs of this rifle along with the Model 1866 Rifles numbers 79863 and 79994 were taken by the Olin Corporation during the 1960s when all three pieces were on loan to the company. The attributions of ownership consequently reflect who their owners were at that time.) The rifle's receiver is engraved with scrollwork enclosing four panel scenes. The characteristics of the ornament which identify it as being done by Ulrich are the exquisitely cut and balanced scrolls which are further embellished with highlight lines cut on

Plate 3: Right receiver detail of the Model 1866 Rifle illustrated in Plate 2. Olin Corporation Photograph, Winchester Arms Collection Archives, Cody Firearms Museum, Buffalo Bill Historical Center, Cody, Wyoming.

Plate 4: Left receiver detail of the Model 1866 Rifle illustrated in Plate 2. Olin Corporation Photograph, Winchester Arms Collection Archives, Cody Firearms Museum, Buffalo Bill Historical Center, Cody, Wyoming.

the curving planes to give them an illusion of depth; the inclusion of finely modelled animal and bird terminals as well as masques within the scrollwork; the use of formally framed panel scenes; and the meticulously crosshatched ground against which the scrollwork is set. The form of the scrollwork and the ground treatment were to remain hallmarks of Herman Ulrich's work throughout most of his working life. The figures of Virtue and Liberty set within niches on, respectively, the right and left forward sections of the receiver, also are indicative of H.L.Ulrich's work, not only from the point of view of their modelling, but also the manner through which they are given a three dimensional quality—the use of cut lines to simulate shadows on the figure of Virtue and the draperies of Liberty, as well as the finely crosshatched backdrops for both figures. The left receiver panel scene or vignette continues the illusion of depth through the placement of the horse, its shading and the gradual softening of the landscape to the horizon line. The figure shooting, as well as the distant mounted figures (presumably Indians), are, however, rather weak in execution. This failing is also evident in the equestrian portrait of General Ulysses S. Grant located in the right rear receiver panel scenes. This portrait does, though, conform to the formal conventions then in use for such work, and its weakness may, therefore, be more a result of those strictures than of the work itself.

By serial number, the next work identified to Ulrich's hand is the Model 1866 Rifle number 28549 (Plates 5 to 8). The rear side sections of the receiver are engraved with simple scrolls (identical in form and execution to those found on the barrel of the preceding rifle number 26283) which enclose

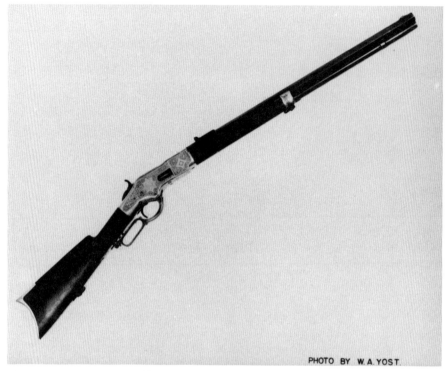

PHOTO BY W.A. YOST

Plate 5: Winchester Model 1866 Rifle, serial number 28549, engraved by Herman L. Ulrich circa 1870. W.A. Yost Photograph, Winchester Arms Collection Archives, Cody Firearms Museum, Buffalo Bill Historical Center, Cody, Wyoming.

blank geometrically formed cartouches. The forward side sections of the receiver are engraved with a four-lobed cartouche flanked at the angles by fleur-de-lis. Apart from the pleasing composition of the work, it is typical of that provided by the Winchester Repeating Arms Company to clients who ordered standard, inexpensively engraved arms. It should be noted, though, that while the engraving is somewhat worn, certain details incorporated in the work demonstrate Ulrich's attention to quality even on products sold at minimal cost. Specifically, Ulrich finely lined the scroll turns and composed them in a fluid manner so that they accentuated the shaped cartouches. The presence of Ulrich's initials engraved on the left hand forward side of the upper tang may, or may not, represent his standard manner of identifying pieces engraved by him during this period.

The two slightly later works by Herman Ulrich that can be identified are the Model 1866 Rifles, serial numbers 79863 (Plates 9 to 11) and 79994 (Plates 12 to 15), which were displayed by the Winchester Repeating Arms Company at the 1873 International Exhibition held in Vienna, Austria. The

Plate 6: Right receiver detail of the Model 1866 illustrated in Plate 5. W.A. Yost Photograph, Winchester Arms Collection Archives, Cody Firearms Museum, Buffalo Bill Historical Center, Cody, Wyoming.

Plate 7: Left receiver detail of the Model 1866 illustrated in Plate 5. W.A. Yost Photograph, Winchester Arms Collection Archives, Cody Firearms Museum, Buffalo Bill Historical Center, Cody, Wyoming.

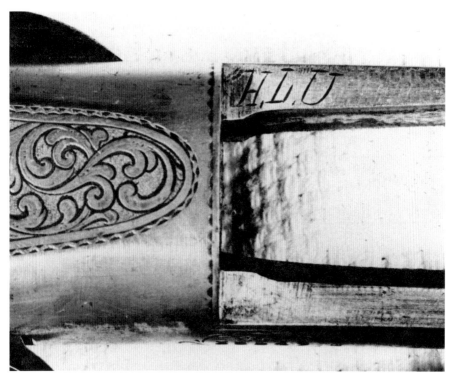

Plate 8: Detail of H.L.Ulrich's signature on the upper receiver tang of the Model 1866 illustrated in Plate 5. W.A. Yost Photograph, Winchester Arms Collection Archives, Cody Firearms Museum, Buffalo Bill Historical Center, Cody, Wyoming.

receiver of the first of these, serial number 79863, is engraved with four relief cut panel scenes enclosed within architectural frames and scrollwork inhabited on the right side with fauna which form an extension of the rear panel scene. While the dress of the hunter depicted in the forward left receiver panel is ambiguous, that of the hunter in the right rear receiver vignette is

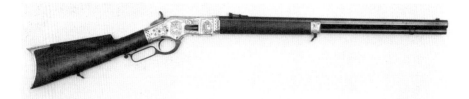

Plate 9: Winchester Model 1866 Rifle, serial number 79863, engraved by H.L.Ulrich for exhibition by the Winchester company at the International Exhibition held in Vienna in 1873. Formerly in the collection of T.H. Hutcheson. Olin Corporation Photograph, Winchester Arms Collection Archives, Cody Firearms Museum, Buffalo Bill Historical Center, Cody, Wyoming.

Plate 10: Right receiver detail of the Model 1866 Rifle illustrated in Plate 9. Olin Corporation Photograph, Winchester Arms Collection Archives, Cody Firearms Museum, Buffalo Bill Historical Center, Cody, Wyoming.

Plate 11: Left receiver detail of the Model 1866 Rifle, illustrated in Plate 9. Olin Corporation Photograph, Winchester Arms Collection Archives, Cody Firearms Museum, Buffalo Bill Historical Center, Cody, Wyoming.

Plate 12: Winchester Model 1866 Rifle, serial number 79994, engraved by H.L.Ulrich for exhibition by the Winchester company at the International Exhibition held in Vienna in 1873. J.M. Peck Collection. Olin Corporation Photograph, Winchester Arms Collection Archives, Cody Firearms Museum, Buffalo Bill Historical Center, Cody, Wyoming.

distinctly European in flavour. As with the preceding example, the illusion of depth has been accentrated by means of shading and the finely crosshatched ground. The incorporation of geometric shapes (quatrefeuilles, circles, swirls, etc.) into the decorative scheme indicated a willingness on the engraver's part to experiment with rather strong border and terminal motifs. In addition, the use of architectural frames, as well as the one hunter's dress, both represent an attempt to decorate this arm in a manner in keeping with its first venue. The forend cap and buttplate tang are engraved simply with scrolls which, along with those on the receiver, are identical in form to the preceding. The barrel, in contrast to the previous example, is unembellished.

Plate 13: Right receiver detail of the Model 1866 Rifle illustrated in Plate 12, Olin Corporation Photograph, Winchester Arms Collection Archives, Cody Firearms Museum, Buffalo Bill Historical Center, Cody, Wyoming.

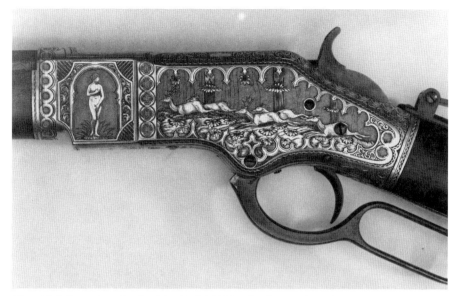

Plate 14: Left receiver detail of the Model 1866 Rifle illustrated in Plate 12, Olin Corporation Photograph, Winchester Arms Collection Archives, Cody Firearms Museum, Buffalo Bill Historical Center, Cody, Wyoming.

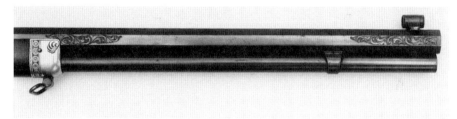

Plate 15: Muzzle detail of the Model 1866 Rifle illustrated in Plate 12, Olin Corporation Photograph, Winchester Arms Collection Archives, Cody Firearms Museum, Buffalo Bill Historical Center, Cody, Wyoming.

The second rifle, serial number 79994, which was exhibited in Vienna, is decorated much in the same manner as number 79863. The receiver is relief engraved with five panel scenes, again enclosed within formal architectural frames.[10] The figure of Virtue first seen on the Model 1866, serial number 26283, now is modelled in relief with further depth again being achieved through shading. While the two circular game scenes chiseled on the right rear receiver are somewhat conventional in form, the placement of the fawn drinking water in the foreground on the larger panel is not only exquisitely done, but also adds considerable depth to the composition. Although the large panel scene of coursing deer on the left side of the receiver achieves a certain degree of depth, its major success is in the simulation of motion through the ascending placement of the deer from rear to front. On this rifle Ulrich not only used geometric motifs for borders and terminals, but also incorporated them into the decorative scheme as a whole. As with both preceding pieces, the ground against which all work is set has been finely crosshatched. The forend cap, buttplate tang and barrel are all engraved with subsidiary scrollwork of identical form to that of the receiver. The decoration of this rifle again is distinctly European in character and demonstrates that the Winchester company specifically tailored the embellishment of exhibition rifles for their potential audience. A pull from another Model 1866 Rifle prepared by Herman Ulrich for the Vienna International Exhibition further substantiates this point, as it illustrates a relief cut hunting scene wherein the hunters are dressed in the European manner and are armed with hunting swords.[11]

Chronologically, the next work to be identified as having been embellished by Herman Ulrich is a Winchester Model 1873 Rifle, serial number 2681, (Plates 16 to 19) which was completed in late January or early February of

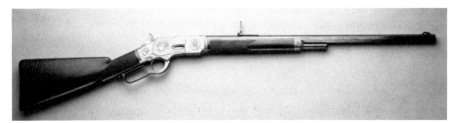

Plate 16: Winchester Model 1873 Rifle, serial number 2681, engraved by H.L.Ulrich. Photograph courtesy of Christie's East, New York.

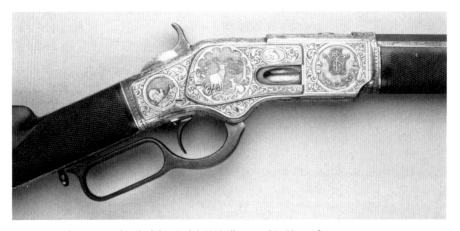

Plate 17: Right receiver detail of the Model 1873 illustrated in Plate 16.

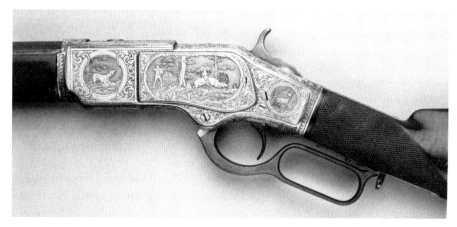

Plate 18: Left receiver detail of the Model 1873 illustrated in Plate 16.

1875.[12] Despite the fact that the receivers of the Model 1873 series were made of iron, as opposed to brass as with the Model 1866, the manner of decoration was continued. The right side of the receiver is engraved with two circular relief cut game scenes, the larger of which has a scalloped interior edge to its surround, and a circular cartouche containing the relief cut monogram WES and the date "Jan. 1st. 1875." The border to this cartouche is enhanced on its right and left sides with scrolls which extend into the panel to terminate in

Plate 19: Detail of the relief cut cartouche on the right receiver of the Model 1873 illustrated in Plate 16.

ribands. In addition to the relief cut scenes, this side of the receiver is further decorated with a small oval panel engraved with a squirrel. The left side of the receiver has three relief cut panels scenes: the forwardmost containing a hound with a downed hare; the centermost, a hunting scene depicting a hunter shooting stags; and that at the rear with a standing doe (which appears to have been startled, as if by the hunter's rifle shot). Apart from the careful delineation of the game, attention should also be called to the detailed treatment of the foliage within the panel scenes. The manner in which this was done remained a consistent factor in Herman Ulrich's work until almost the end of his working career. The scrollwork cut on the receiver mirrors that encountered on prior examples. The forward and rear borders of the receiver are cut with bands of anthemion ornament, a feature which was to recur in later work. Interestingly, the screw heads and tips were engraved en suite with the decoration surrounding them. This feature did not recur in Ulrich's work, probably because once a screw is loosened it never resets in the same position. Thus, the engraving does not realign with its surroundings (as has happened in this case). While the barrel is undecorated, the forend cap and buttplate tang are engraved with subsidiary scrollwork. The face of the buttplate is engraved with chequering. In contrast to the preceding pieces, the ground against which the panels and scrolls are set is not lined but rather pointille. A comparison of this ground with that encountered on the hammer of the Colt New Line Revolver described below reveals that it was executed by the same tool augmented by hand. Interestingly, although this rifle was built and engraved during the period that H.L.Ulrich was the sole engraver for the Winchester company, the lower tang is stamped with the mark of John Ulrich who was then employed in the firm's Gun Assembly Room. The presence of this mark on a work which is quite evidently the product of H.L.Ulrich's hand, while perplexing and definitely misleading, represents an example of John Ulrich's practice to stamp pieces which were not his with his signature die.[13]

Comparison of this rifle with one engraved a year later by John Ulrich in an almost identical manner, graphically demonstrates the differences between the two brothers' work.[14] While Herman was able to endow his game portraits with vitality, John Ulrich's depictions of game are two dimensional in character. His comprehension of anatomy and composition were also not as fully developed. In consequence the game scenes he engraved are somewhat awkward. A more telling characteristic of John Ulrich's work, both on his copy of serial number 2681 and other pieces, is the flacid nature of the scrollwork and the almost total reliance upon the use of a punch dot ground.

Due to a progressive reduction in the call for engraving work by the Winchester company beginning in 1874, Herman Ulrich began to establish business relationships with a number of other clients.[15] The most notable of these were the American Bank Note Company of New York and the Colt's

Patent Fire Arms Manufacturing Company in Hartford. Although little is known of his work for the former firm, one major piece has survived from his association with Colt: a .30 caliber New Line Revolver, serial number 5018 (Plates 20 to 24). Aside from its value as a testament to Ulrich's capabilities, this little revolver is of importance because it was the engraver's personal sidearm.

Initially, the most remarkable feature of this revolver is its distinctive finish. The combination of the gold plated frame, blued cylinder and bright barrel forms a very colorful as well as aesthetically pleasing appearance, which, though partially seen in the previous Winchester rifles, is more fully developed and defined here. The frame of the revolver is engraved with scrollwork inhabited by fox, wyvern and hound's heads. Along either side of the sighting groove cut into the top strap over the cylinder, the scrollwork is divided by a plain quatrefeuille panel. The bearing surfaces of the grip backstrap and inner grip are finely chequered as are the forward sides of the trigger housing. The point where the backstrap joins the frame is engraved with a panel of

Plate 20: Colt New Line Revolver, serial number 5018, engraved and gold inlaid by H.L.Ulrich for his personal use. Ulrich Family Collection.

Plate 21: Overall top view of the Colt New Line Revolver illustrated in Plate 20.

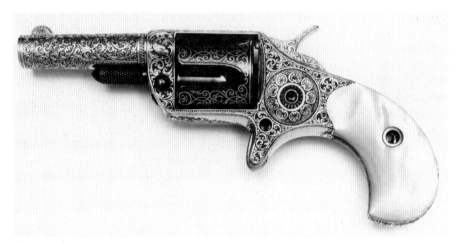

Plate 22: Overall left-hand view of the Colt New Line Revolver illustrated in Plate 20.

anthemion ornament. The lower strap of the frame is engraved with a simple panel of scrollwork. With the exception of the latter, all the scroll engraving is set against a crosshatched ground. The right side of the frame is also engraved with a relief cut medallion containing a squirrel sitting on its haunches. The sideplate located on the left side of the receiver is engraved with circular bands of acanthus and anthemion ornament. The hammer is engraved on its right, left and rear sides with scrolls set against a pointille ground. This ground in part was done with a circular punch with the remainder having been hand cut. The cylinder is inlaid with interlacing scroll ornament, while the edges of the cylinder flutes are engraved with an undulating line border set with dots at regular intervals. The rear circumference of the cylinder is inlaid with narrow gold border band. The barrel is chiselled with formally composed scrollwork, and the muzzle and breech are bordered respectively with bands of anthemion and acanthus ornament. The top of the barrel is engraved in old English letters with the manufacturer's name, Colt, within a lobed cartouche which is bordered to the front and rear with chiselled arabesques.

Plate 23: Overall bottom view of the Colt New Line Revolver illustrated in Plate 20.

Plate 24: Detail of the relief cut panels located on the right frame side of the Colt New Line Revolver illustrated in Plate 20.

The decoration of the revolver, in particular the type of scrollwork, its placement and the use of a crosshatched ground, is identical to that encountered on a limited number of Colt revolvers produced between 1875 and late 1879.[16] It is highly probable that most, if not all, of these pistols were engraved by Herman Ulrich under contract let by the Colt company.

During the latter half of the 1870s Ulrich apparently directed his attentions increasingly toward the stock market. The degree of this interest and his success in it can be best demonstrated by his purchase of the New Haven Stock Exchange seat of N.S. Roberts and Company in late January or early February of 1880, with E.P. Atkinson as a minority shareholder.[17] The firm of H.L.Ulrich & Company operated in New Haven until September of 1880, when Ulrich moved to Brooklyn, New York, where he purchased a seat on that city's Stock Exchange and set up business at Number 4 Myrtle Avenue (Plate 25).[18] Despite the rigors of his new profession, or perhaps as a release from them, Ulrich continued to indulge his earlier vocation on occasion. In 1883 or 1884, he produced two engraving plates for the American Bank Note Company. One of these, a three-quarter view of an elk standing in a pond set amidst lush foliage (Plate 26) proved to be quite popular and remains to this day one of the company's stock images.[19] In 1889, a protracted bout with "pulmmory disease" caused Ulrich (Plate 27) to sell his stock exchange seat and retire.[20] A confidential report prepared by the Brooklyn City Bank at this time states simply that he had "accumulated a sufficient fortune to meet his every need for the next fifty years, should in the unlikely event he survive that length of time."[21]

Upon retirement, Ulrich returned to Hartford where he re-established a contractual relationship with the Colt company.[22] The most important piece which resulted from this renewed association is a Large Frame Lightning Magazine Rifle, serial number 5164 (Plates 28 to 45) which was presented to His Excellency, General Don Porfirio Diaz, President of the United States of

BROOKLYN STOCK EXCHANGE.

H. L. ULRICH & CO.

STOCK BROKERS,

No. 4 Myrtle Avenue,

COR. FULTON STREET.   BROOKLYN, N. Y.

Plate 25: Trade card for H.L.Ulrich & Company, No. 4 Myrtle Avenue, Brooklyn, New York. Ulrich Family Collection.

STAG

Plate 26: Vignette of a standing elk engraved by H.L.Ulrich circa 1883 or 1884 for the American Bank Note Company. American Bank Note Company Archives.

Mexico by the New York arms dealer Hartley & Graham in early 1891.[23] In the combination of its finish (rosewood stocks, gold plated receiver and silver plated barrel as well as magazine tube), this rifle is as striking as Ulrich's personal Colt New Line Revolver. The quality and complexity of its engraving also is of equal standing. The receiver is engraved with very tight scrollwork enclosed within a variety of borders, as well as eight panel scenes and one oval medallion deeply relief cut with the general's monogram. The major panel scenes engraved on the receiver are as follows: horseman shooting a buffalo (right center side); a standing elk (left forward side); a pointer (left center side); and the Mexican eagle (left rear side). Subsidiary vignettes include the depictions of two partridges (right forward side); a retriever's head (over the barrel breech); and a grouse (upper receiver tang). In addition, the Colt Patent Fire Arms Manufacturing Company's symbol of the rampant colt is engraved on top of the bolt cover.

Interestingly, a detailed examination of the panel scenes and subsidiary vignettes indicates that two of the elements were executed by a different hand. Both the horseman and buffalo scene, as well as the rampant colt medallion, are amateurishly done on comparison with the other work. In particular, they display a lack of modelling, knowledge of anatomy and an absence of depth which is quite unlike that found in Herman Ulrich's work.

Plate 27: Photograph of H.L.Ulrich taken circa 1889 or 1890. Ulrich Family Collection.

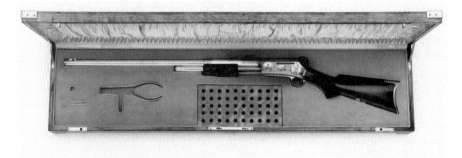

Plate 28: Colt Lightning Magazine Rifle, serial number 5164, engraved by H.L.Ulrich for the firm of Hartley & Graham which presented it in 1891 to His Excellency, General Don Porfirio Diaz, President of the United States of Mexico. Douglas Arms Collection (Inv. No. D63), Royal Military College of Canada, Kingston, Ontario.

Plate 29: Overall right hand view of the Colt Lightning Magazine Rifle illustrated in Plate 28.

Plate 30: Right receiver detail of the Colt Lightning Magazine Rifle illustrated in Plate 28.

The figures of the horseman and buffalo are almost cartoonish in nature, especially when one notes that the buffalo has only one horn. Though some attempt to depict depth was made through the use of shading, the composition is entirely two dimensional and vapid. Likewise, the rampant colt lacks depth and realism. When the treatment of the animal figures contained in these two elements is compared with that of the elk or pointer, the disparity between the work becomes quite pronounced. Likewise, the detail accorded foliage even in the small vignettes is much greater than that seen in either the horseman and buffalo or rampant colt depictions. In addition, it should be noted that circumstantial evidence supports the conclusion that the horseman and buffalo scene was cut after the other decoration was done.

While it could be understood if the rampant colt design was left for an apprentice to do, it is incomprehensible that a major element of the decoration would be assigned to an understudy. Thus, the origin of at least the horseman and buffalo scene must be sought elsewhere. Comparison of it with the work done by Cuno Helfricht who was in charge of the Colt company's engraving shop at the time, reveals such marked similarities that it can be safely attributed to him.[24] The reasons for Helfricht's participation in the decoration of this rifle unfortunately cannot be determined now, but it is known

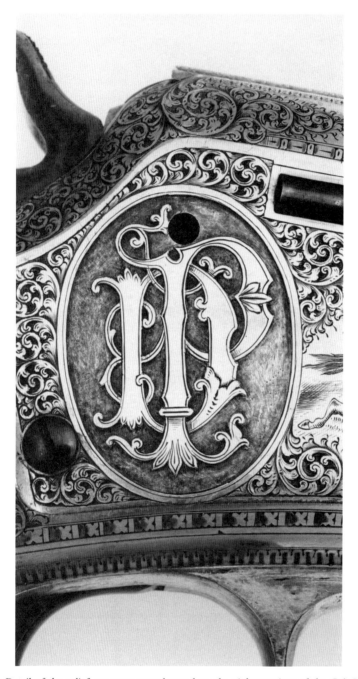

Plate 31: Detail of the relief cut monogram located on the right receiver of the Colt Lightning Magazine Rifle illustrated in Plate 28.

Plate 32: Detail of the mounted hunter and buffalo vignette believed to have been engraved by Cuno Helfricht on the right receiver of the Colt Lightning Magazine Rifle illustrated in Plate 28.

that he and Ulrich did not get along and it may, therefore, have been an attempt by Helfricht to put his imprimatur on one of Ulrich's projects.[25]

The decoration of the trigger guard, lower receiver, buttplate tang, barrel breech, barrel muzzle and the point where the barrel section changes from octagonal to round, consists solely of scrollwork bordered where appropriate with bands of anthemion or geometric ornament. As with the scrollwork found on the receiver, the ground is finely lined.

If one discounts the horseman and buffalo as well as the rampant colt vignettes, the content and execution of the work evidenced in this rifle must place it among the finest of Herman Ulrich's work. It was perhaps in recognition of this that he signed the piece with his initials in the ground of the Diaz monogram both between the lower right terminal of the letter P and the sway on the bow of the letter D, and to the left of the letter D's vertical member (Plate 45).

The presence of the border bands composed of multiple X's, crenelated geometric ornament, the placement of tear drop accents on plain ground

Plate 33: Detail of the partridge vignette engraved on the forward right receiver of the Colt Lightning Magazine Rifle illustrated in Plate 28.

bordering scrollwork and sworled scrolls such as those found on the trigger-guard bow, seriously bring into question the origin of a pencil design sketch previously attributed to Cuno Helfricht (Plate 46). In addition to the new motifs noted above, the sketch displays all the other characteristic hallmarks of Ulrich's work found in the Colt New Line Revolver as well as the Colt and Winchester rifles discussed previously: namely, the creation of depth within vignettes through the placement of figures and the use of foliage or landscape backdrops, the use of relief work as well as lined ground, and the form of some of the scrollwork. The points of comparison with Helfricht's work, on the other hand, are minimal. Thus, this drawing should be considered a design

Plate 34: Vignette of a pointer's head engraved on the receiver breech ring of the Colt Lightning Magazine Rifle illustrated in Plate 28.

Plate 35: Rampant colt logo engraved on the dust cover of the Colt Lightning Magazine Rifle illustrated in Plate 28.

Plate 36: Vignette of a grouse engraved on the upper receiver tang of the Colt Lightning Magazine Rifle illustrated in Plate 28.

Plate 37: Left receiver of the Colt Lightning Magazine Rifle illustrated in Plate 28.

Plate 38: Vignette of a standing elk engraved on the forward left receiver of the Colt Lightning Magazine Rifle illustrated in Plate 28.

Plate 39: Vignette of a pointer engraved on the left receiver of the Colt Lightning Magazine Rifle illustrated in Plate 28.

Plate 40: Vignette of the Mexican Eagle engraved on the left rear receiver of the Colt Lightning Magazine Rifles illustrated in Plate 28.

Plate 41: Trigger guard and lower receiver of the Colt Lightning Magazine Rifle illustrated in Plate 28.

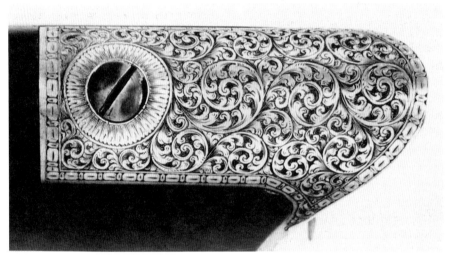

Plate 42: Detail of the upper buttplate tang of the Colt Lightning Magazine Rifle illustrated in Plate 28.

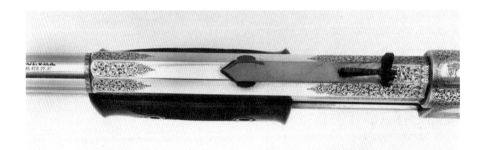

Plate 43: Octagonal barrel section of the Colt Lightning Magazine Rifle illustrated in Plate 28.

Plate 44: Muzzle detail of the Colt Lightning Magazine Rifle illustrated in Plate 28.

exercise done by Ulrich for the development of engraving designs, possibly to be executed in the Colt engraving shop.

The decoration of the Diaz Colt Rifle also brings into question Helfricht's supposed authorship of the engraving found on a series of Colt Double Barrel Rifles and Model 1878 Shotguns produced during 1878 and 1879, as they exhibit characteristics more in keeping with Ulrich's work rather than Helfricht's.[26]

Plate 45: Highlighted detail of the signatures engraved in the background of the right receiver monogram panel on the Colt Lightning Magazine Rifle illustrated in Plate 28.

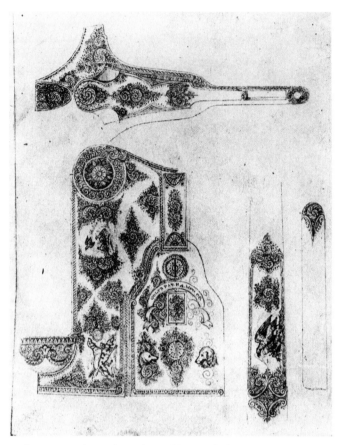

Plate 46: Pencil engraving design for Colt Double Barrel Shotguns preserved in the Helfricht Family Papers. E.I. Blomstrann Photograph.

Though a formal relationship with Colt was to last until 1899, Ulrich renewed his association with the Winchester company prior to August 22 of 1897.[27]

During the initial period of this second tenure with the Winchester Repeating Arms Company, Ulrich's primary task was to develop new designs for the firm's standardized engraving styles.[28] The ultimate result of this work was the production of a series of revised game and hunting scenes which were refinements of those he drew under an earlier contract for the company's Highly Finished Arms catalog issued in October of 1897 (Plate 47). The character of this work may be best described as a synthesized restatement of what he had done earlier. There was, however, no recidivism in it, for he continued to experiment with the creation of depth through the use of shadows and the presentation of game as well as foliage with finely lined grounds. He

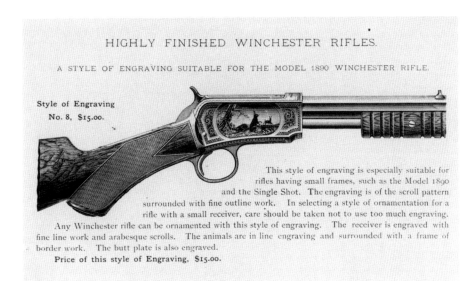

HIGHLY FINISHED WINCHESTER RIFLES.

A STYLE OF ENGRAVING SUITABLE FOR THE MODEL 1890 WINCHESTER RIFLE.

Style of Engraving
No. 8, $15.00.

This style of engraving is especially suitable for
rifles having small frames, such as the Model 1890
and the Single Shot. The engraving is of the scroll pattern
surrounded with fine outline work. In selecting a style of ornamentation for a
rifle with a small receiver, care should be taken not to use too much engraving.
Any Winchester rifle can be ornamented with this style of engraving. The receiver is engraved with
fine line work and arabesque scrolls. The animals are in line engraving and surrounded with a frame of
border work. The butt plate is also engraved.
Price of this style of Engraving, $15.00.

Plate 47: Engraving style Number 8 illustrated on page 18 of the Winchester Repeating Arms
Company's Highly Finished Arms Catalogue issued in October of 1897. This design together with
those illustrated on pages 4 and 5 are the work of H.L.Ulrich. Winchester Arms Collection
Archives, Cody Firearms Museum, Buffalo Bill Historical Center, Cody, Wyoming.

also introduced to his repertoire a simplified scroll which was rather elegant
and more modern in nature. To reduce production costs, the designs he developed for the Winchester company did not incorporate lined grounds for scroll
work but rather the easily done pointille ground. Special commissions, however, continued to be executed with finely lined grounds. One distinguishing
characteristic of the designs developed by Herman Ulrich was the manner in
which he utilized the planes of a rifle's receiver to accent the design.
Although this utilization of curving planes had been evident as early as the
1870's, the sharply defined horizontal reduction of the Model 1895's receiver
width below the bolt provided him with considerable challenge. In contrast
to his brother John and the majority of the Winchester company's other
engravers, Herman Ulrich extended his scrollwork into the concave section
and modified its form so that the work reflected the symmetry of the section
(Plate 48).

Despite his ever-increasing commitment to the Winchester company,
Herman Ulrich continued to accept other commissions. In late 1901, he
designed and engraved a vignette of a miner for the American Bank Note
Company which was later used by that firm in the production of the Dawson
City Mining Court Law Stamp (Plate 49).[29]

In 1903, Ulrich engraved two Model 1903 Self-Loading Rifles for the
Winchester company which was destined for presentation by the firm to

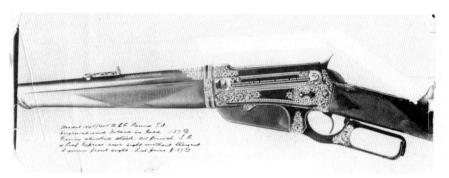

Plate 48: Winchester Model 1895 Sporting Rifle engraved by H.L.Ulrich circa 1900. Winchester Repeating Arms Company Photograph, Winchester Arms Collection Archives, Cody Firearms Museum, Buffalo Bill Historical Center, Cody, Wyoming.

Emperor Manelek II of Ethiopia.[30] The records concerning these rifles indicate that they were fitted with carved fancy pistol grip stocks and that they were

Plate 49: Hand-painted essay for the Yukon-Dawson Mining Court Law Stamp of 1903 which was produced by the American Bank Note Company. The center vignette of the miner was designed and engraved by H.L.Ulrich in 1901. American Bank Note Company Archives, sold Christie's Robson Lowe, New York, September 13, 1990, Lot 2131.

finished in a combination of nickel and gilt. The receivers, barrels and furniture were engraved at a cost of $15 with an additional charge being levied for the engraving of the following two-line inscription on the bottom of each receiver:

MANELEK 2
EMPEROR OF ETHIOPIA

The present whereabouts of these rifles and, indeed, whether or not they still exist are unfortunately unknown.

The possible form of the Manelek II rifles' decoration may perhaps be gauged by another Winchester Model 1903 Sporting Rifle (Plate 50) which was engraved by Ulrich in 1904.[31] The design encountered on this piece is of interest in that the ground against which the vignette as well as foliate scrollwork are set has been relieved and very finely lined.

In 1904, Ulrich moved from Hartford to New Haven and entered into an exclusive contractual relationship with Winchester which was to last until his retirement as a contractor on December 21, 1923.[32]

After 1904, Herman Ulrich's responsibilities were increased to include the supervision of the factory's engraving shop and the training of apprentices, in addition to the continued refinement of standard engraving styles. By 1910, the engraving shop had greatly expanded its selection of standard work, while at the same time retaining certain forms which had considerable popular following. The value of H.L.Ulrich's work at the time can perhaps be best demonstrated by the fact that his engraving of a monogram in May of 1910 cost the company $5 and was, therefore, charged out at $12.50 ($2 more than the cost of a standard Model 1906).[33] Though such work was curtailed by the exigencies of wartime production, it is known that Herman Ulrich personally engraved one major commission in early 1916: a Pattern 14 Infantry rifle which was presented to King George V of England by the J.P. Morgan &

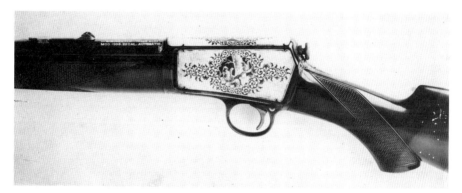

Plate 50: Winchester Model 1903 Sporting Rifle, serial number 21816, engraved by H.L.Ulrich in 1904. Winchester Repeating Arms Company Photograph, Winchester Arms Collection Archives, Cody Firearms Museum, Buffalo Bill Historical Center, Cody, Wyoming.

Company of New York City, the cost of which was set at $75. The top of the receiver over the barrel breech was inlaid in gold with the royal arms of the United Kingdom and the monarch's monogram was likewise rendered in relief in two colors of gold on the magazine floor plate. Apart from these embellishments, the contract only called for the stock to be of the finest walnut and the steel components to be highly polished and blued.[34]

In January of 1918 the Engraving Department was temporarily closed and Ulrich, together with his staff, was transferred to the Gun Assembly Shop so that war orders could be promptly fulfilled.[35]

After World War I, Herman Ulrich's contributions to the Winchester company lessened. It is known that he continued to instruct apprentices and supervise the activities of the engraving shop, but the call for new designs was apparently more or less abandoned.

The final footnote to Herman Ulrich's career at the Winchester Repeating Arms occurred in 1923 when he was presented with a gold Long Service Medal struck from the die he had cut for the firm many years earlier.[36] In a very real sense, this presentation was a fitting conclusion to his association with the company.

About 1929, Ulrich returned again to Hartford and lived with his brother George. On March 10, 1937, Herman Leslie Ulrich died at the age of 90.[37]

NOTES

1. "the appearance of evidence being necessarily so various to every one of us . . . ." Jonathan Richardson the Elder, *The Connoisseur* (London: 1719); quoted in Sir John Pope-Hennessey, *The Study and Criticism of Italian Sculpture* (New York: Metropolitan Museum of Art, 1980), p. 12.

2. Pope-Hennessey, *The Study and Criticism of Italian Sculpture*, p. 22.

3. This misattribution has been the result not only of the superficial resemblance of H.L.Ulrich's work to that produced by his brothers, but also, R.L. Wilson's appraisal of his abilities in *The Book of Winchester Engraving* (Los Angeles: Beinfeld Publishing, Inc., 1975), p. 83.

4. See in particular the following descriptions of the Winchester Model 1866 Rifle serial number 79994 and Model 1873Rifle serial number 2681, together with Footnotes 10 and 13.

5. All the material relating to the family history of the Ulrichs is based upon documents and other papers in the possession of Dorothy Ulrich, who is Herman L. Ulrich's niece.

6. The Hartford City directory for 1867 lists Herman Ulrich as an engraver boarding at his parents' home.

7. Ulrich's salary is based upon entries contained in the Winchester Repeating Arms Company's *Payroll Book* (March 1869-March 31, 1871) [Private Collection], while the date of his employment is preserved in the Miscellaneous Records, Winchester Repeating Arms Company, Winchester Arms Collection Archives, Cody Firearms Museum, Buffalo Bill Historical Center, Cody, Wyoming.

8. Winchester Repeating Arms Company *Gun Contractors Ledger*, pp. 74 and 75. Winchester Arms Collection Archives, Cody Firearms Museum, Buffalo Bill Historical Center, Cody, Wyoming. The payroll books (March 1869-March 31, 1871 and April 1871-May 3, 1873) and *Gun Contractors Ledger* allow the employment records of Herman, Conrad and John Ulrich to be reconstructed as follows:

    A. Herman Ulrich
        Sole Engraving Contractor July 29, 1870 to March 1871
        Engraving Contractor (with his brother Conrad) April 1871 to March 1874
        Sole Engraving Contractor May 1874 to May 29, 1875
    B. Conrad Ulrich
        Engraving Contractor (with his brother Herman) April 1871 to March 7, 1874
    C. John Ulrich
        Employed in Gun Assembly Room
        Stock Maker and Apprentice Engraver to Conrad April 1871 to May 3, 1871
        Employed in Gun Assembly Room May 3, 1873 to June 1875
        Engraving Contractor June 1875 to approximately 1910 (the latter part of his career
        primarily was involved with wood carving, etc.).

9. Wilson, *The Book of Winchester Engraving*, pp. 84-89.

10. It should be noted that the presence of Conrad F. Ulrich's signature stamp on a Winchester firearm made during the period of April 1871 to March 1874, does not necessarily prove that such an arm was personally engraved by him. Rather, it reflects the traditional German practice of marking products with the name of the prime contractor and his assumption of credit for all work produced under him. During H.L.Ulrich's tenure as chief engraving contractor the practice was abandoned. It was, however, reintroduced on a limited scale by John Ulrich after the latter became chief engraver for the Winchester company in late 1875.

11. This pull is preserved in the Ulrich Family papers.

12. Winchester Repeating Arms Company Model 1873 Serial Number Register Volume 1 records that number 2681 was received in the company's warehouse on February 20, 1875. It was recorded as being a Rifle fitted with a 24″ octagonal barrel, chequered XXXO stock, set trigger, silver front sight, "Engraved, gold etc. . ." The rifle was shipped under Order Number 2554 on

February 20, 1875. Model 1873 Serial Number Register Volume 1, Winchester Arms Collection Archives, Cody Firearms Museum, Buffalo Bill Historical Center, Cody, Wyoming.

13. Confirmation for this assertion is to be found in the following letter:

May 5, 1884

H.L.Ulrich & Co. / Number 4 Myrtle Avenue / Brooklyn, New York

Samual T. Baker
Oraville [sic], California

Dear Sir

Yours of the 21st has been received. The news you relate concerning the marking of your rifles is most distressing. I have however been informed reliably that Mr John Ulrich has adoped the fashion of stamping Winchester Repeating Arms Company rifles &c with his touch mark when they are sent to that company's works for any reason.

Should you wish redress, I am positive that Gov Winchester's successor Mr William Converse will be able to assist you.

Your obt servent

H.L.Ulrich

14. For illustrations of the rifle engraved by John Ulrich, see Wilson, *The Book of Winchester Engraving*, p. 151.

15. This statement is based not only upon the diminished demand for this work as reflected in the company's *Gun Contractors Ledger* but, also, the reduced number of engraved arms recorded in the company's Serial Number Registers. In addition, a notation in the archives of the America Bank Note Company dated November, [?], 1874, indicates Ulrich did some unspecified engraving work for them prior to that date.

16. For example, see the Colt New Line Revolvers illustrated in Wilson, *The Book of Colt Engraving* (Los Angeles: Wallace Beinfeld Publishing, Inc., 1974), p. 199.

17. Records of R.G. Dun & Company, Connecticut, Volume 41, p. 402. R.G. Dun & Co. Collection, Baker Library, Harvard University.

18. Trade card preserved in the Ulrich Family Papers.

19. American Bank Note Company Archives.

20. Confidential Report prepared by "E.D." in February of 1889 for the Brooklyn City Bank.

21. Confidential Report prepared by "E.D." in February of 1889 for the Brooklyn City Bank.

22. Ulrich re-established his residence in Hartford at his parents' house (14 Alden Street).

23. Douglas Arms Collection, Royal Military College of Canada, Kingston, Ontario, Inventory Number D63.

24. For example, see the Colt Burgess Rifle, serial number 285, in Wilson, *The Book of Colt Engraving*, p. 268.

25. The trying relationship between Helfricht and Ulrich is noted in Wilson, *The Book of Winchester Engraving*, p. 84.

26. For example see Wilson, *The Book of Colt Engraving*, pp. 265 and 267.

27. The records of the Winchester Repeating Arms Company indicate that Ulrich formally became a contract employee on August 22, 1897, but had had at least two work commissions during the year prior.

28. The hiring of H.L.Ulrich as senior engraving contractor was done on the direct orders of Thomas G. Bennett, President of the Winchester Repeating Arms Company, who was seriously concerned about the deterioration of the company's engraving options developed and executed by John Ulrich (T.G. Bennett, Manuscript Diary, notes for April 5, 1897 and August 21, 1897 [Bennett Family Papers]). The demotion of John Ulrich and his gradual phasing out over the next decade probably was the cause of some additional animosity between the brothers.

29. American Bank Note Company Archives, sold Christie's New York, September 13, 1990, Lot 2131.

30. Winchester Repeating Arms Company *Special Order Book*, p. 112 and Model 1903 Serial Number Register Volume 1. Winchester Arms Collection Archives, Cody Firearms Museum, Buffalo Bill Historical Center, Cody, Wyoming.

31. Due to the difference in cost between this rifle and the Manelek II rifles it is highly likely that the latter did not have relieved grounds to the engraved vignettes and scrollwork. Model 1903 Serial Number Register Volume 1. Winchester Arms Collection Archives, Cody Firearms Museum, Buffalo Bill Historical Center, Cody, Wyoming.

32. Records of the Winchester Repeating Arms Company, Engraving-Ulrich, Herman L. Winchester Arms Collection Archives, Cody Firearms Museum, Buffalo Bill Historical Center, Cody, Wyoming.

33. Winchester Repeating Arms Company *Special Order Book*, p. 155 and Winchester Repeating Arms Company Catalogue Number 76, Issued June, 1910, p. 73.

34. Letter dated February 6, 1916, from J.P. Morgan & Company, to H.F. Beebe, Head of Foreign Sales, Winchester Repeating Arms Company, with Beebe's and John E. Otterson's notations. Winchester Arms Collection Archives, Cody Firearms Museum, Buffalo Bill Historical Center, Cody, Wyoming.

35. Records of the Winchester Repeating Arms Company. Winchester Arms Collection Archives, Cody Firearms Museum, Buffalo Bill Historical Center, Cody, Wyoming.

36. The die for this medal was cut by Ulrich in October of 1912.

37. See endnote 5.

Cody Firearms Museum Advisory Board

Cody Firearms Members

Mr. Paul A. Boyd

Mr. Leo H. Bradshaw, Jr.

Mr. & Mrs. Edward A. Brandhorst

Mr. & Mrs. David B. Brasfield

Mr. Richard Bresson

Mr. & Mrs. Michael L. Brinkmann

Mr. Dennis C. Brooks

Mr. Jack Brown

Mr. Albert D. Buckingham

Mr. Kirk Budd

Mr. Leon Budginas

Mr. Fred R. Burr

Mr. W. L. Burr

Mr. Robert J. Burton

Mr. & Mrs. Michael J. Cairns

Mr. & Mrs. Ray C. Camp

Mr. John Campbell

Mr. Keith W. Campbell

Mr. & Mrs. Robert A. Campbell

Mr. Vincent Capone

Mr. & Mrs. Richard C. Capps

Dr. Paul Carney

Mr. Larry W. Carpenter

Mr. & Mrs. Robert C. Carter

Mr. Jerry F. Cermack

Mr. Chester E. Chellman

Mr. Michael Cherok

Mr. Kevin P. Cherry

Dr. Anthony J. Cipriano

Mr. & Mrs. Mike Claphan

Mr. Michael P. Clark

Mr. Peyton C. Clark, Jr. &
Mr. Vince McMahon

Mr. John R. Clarke

Mr. Randy Clifford

Mr. Steven B. Coates

Mr. Leigh F. Coffin

Mr. & Mrs. Leigh M. Coffin

Collectible Arms International Inc.

Mr. David F. Condon

Mr. & Mrs. Richard M. Conger

Mr. & Mrs. Clayton E. Cooper

Mr. & Mrs. Orvel Cooper

Mr. Liscom Cox

Mr. Donald L. Criswell

Mr. & Mrs. John P. Cunningham

Mr. Tommy Dabbs

Mr. R. Nathan Davis &
Ms. Thresa Stroud

Mr. Buddy DeBarr

Mr. Christian DeGuigne, IV

Mr. John C. Denner

Mr. Les Dillman

Mr. & Mrs. Thomas B. Dintruff

Dixie Gun Works

Mr. & Mrs. Donald B. Dobb

Mr. Bob Domecq

Mr. Keith Doyle

Mr. & Mrs. D. M. Dreher

Thomas and Connie Dunn

Mr. & Mrs. Charles E. DuPont

Dr. & Dr. Russell R. Dutcher

Mr. Les A. Dvorak

Mr. Walter C. Earl

Mr. & Mrs. John Edmondson

Mr. & Mrs. Donald R. Edwards

Mr. James E. Elliott-Forster

Mr. Richard D. Ellsworth

Mr. John English

Mr. & Mrs. Peter E. Erickson

Mr. Norbert Ertel

Mr. Olin C. Ervine

Mr. & Mrs. Lloyd I. Evans

Mr. & Mrs. Thomas L. Evans, Sr.

Mr. & Mrs. William L. Evans

Floyd and Robert Everhart

Mr. Robert M. Ezzell

Mr. Jeff Faintich

Mr. Don Farlow

Mr. & Mrs. Paul Ferrara

Mr. Steven P. Fjestad

Mr. & Mrs. David G. Flurkey

Mr. & Mrs. Jerry L. Fountain

Mr. John E. Fox

Mr. & Mrs. Fred France

Mr. & Mrs. Wallace W. Francis, Jr.

Mr. Mort Friedman

Mr. & Mrs. Paul I. Friedrich

Mr. Douglas Ray Fulkerson

Mr. & Mrs. James H. Fuquay, Jr.

Mr. & Mrs. Chris Fye

Mr. Jim Gamans

Mr. John R. Gangel

Mr. James M. Garland

Mr. Steven N. Gerhardt

Mr. Humbert Ghirlanda

Mr. Charles Gibbens

Mr. Max Gibson

Mr. David Owen Gilberg

Mr. & Mrs. Michael L. Ginn

Mr. John Girard

Mr. & Mrs. James P. Goergen

Mr. Arthur J. Gogan

Mr. William T. Goodman

Mr. Tulane Gordon, III

Mr. Floyd D. Gottwald, Jr.

Mr. Scott Graham

Mr. William Gray

Mr. Warren Greatbatch

Mr. Arthur F. Green

Mr. & Mrs. Don Grove

Mr. & Mrs. James R. Grueter

Mr. & Mrs. James G. Guindon

Mr. Len Guldman

Guns Plus

Mr. & Mrs. Tommy B. Haas

Mr. Charles S. Hackett

Mr. W. P. Hallstein

Mr. Marty Halpern

Mr. Gary Hamilton

Mr. Hal Hamilton

Mr. & Mrs. Richard Hammer

Mr. Clifford L. Hansen

Mr. John R. Hansen, Jr.

Mr. Douglas Hanson

Mrs. Fredric A. Harris

Mr. John L. Harris

Dr. James W. Hartig

Mr. William L. Harvey

Mr. David Haviar

Mr. & Mrs. John Hawk

Mr. Bud Haynes

Mr. Wayne Head

Dr. Bruce Heischober

Dr. & Mrs. Ladd L. Heldenbrand

Mr. Bill Henley &
  Mr. Bill R. Combs

Mr. A. G. Herman, III

Mr. Phillip E. Hiatt

Mr. William V. Hice

Mr. Toby Hildabrand

Mr. & Mrs. Glenn J. Hockett

Mr. J. Davis Hodsden

Mr. Paul D. Hoffman &
  Mr. Jerry Eudy

Mr. & Mrs. Monte Hofstrand

Mr. & Mrs. Reginald R. Holloway

Ray and Linda House

Mr. Edwin R. Hull

Mr. Christian Humbert

Mr. & Mrs. Russell A. Hunter

Mr. Mac C. Jensen

Mr. & Mrs. Carl D. Johnson

Mr. & Mrs. Don Johnson

Mr. & Mrs. Larry W. Jones

Mr. & Mrs. Springer Jones

Mr. David Kahanek

Mr. Braden B. Kane

Mr. Leland Kassell

Mr. Stanley Kellert

Mr. John A. Kieft

Mr. Dave Kinsey

Mr. Bruce W. Kirk

Mr. Kurtis Kirk

Dr. Gerald Klaz

Mr. Kenneth L. Knighten

Mr. Phil Knowles

Mr. J. W. Koch

Mr. Keith Kristjanson

Mr. Stephen Krumm

Mr. & Mrs. Ronald F. Kudryk

Mr. William Kugler

Mr. & Mrs. Edward D. Kukowski

Mr. Roger Kurtz

Mr. John A. Lamson

Mr. Eddie Land

Mr. John M. Lang

Mr. & Mrs. Larry Leach

Mr. Robert M. Lee

Mr. Maurice Lefore

Legendary Guns of the West

Mr. & Mrs. Clark Linders

Mr. & Mrs. John P. Littig

Mr. & Mrs. Donald H. Littman

Mr. Jonathan W. Locke

Mr. Cliff Logan

Mr. Dick Loper

Mr. Mitchell L. Luksich

Mr. Buz Lundgren

Mr. & Mrs. John N. Maddux

Mr. & Mrs. John Madl

Mr. John Maher

Mr. Carl Malkmus

Mr. John J. Malloy

Mr. Robert Maloy

Mr. John Manganiello

Mr. & Mrs. Robert A. Manganiello

Mr. Frank Marcella

Mr. Peter E. Marcovicci

Mr. Hank Marquardt

Dr. & Mrs. William M. Marsh

Mr. Vaughn Masthoff

Mr. Rodney R. McCallum

Mr. & Mrs. Joe B. McCune

Mr. Joseph D. McDaniel

Mr. Lyle McDermott

Mr. & Mrs. Fred B. McDonald

Mr. & Mrs. R. Bruce McDowell

Mr. Jim E. McGhee

Mr. & Mrs. George H. McKeen

Mr. Hugh S. McLean

Mr. & Mrs. Lawrence C. Means

Mr. Joe Melanson

Dr. Daniel H. Menser

Mr. & Mrs. Le Roy Merz

Mr. & Mrs. Don Michel

Mr. Garry Miller

Mr. John F. Miller

Mr. Wayne A. Miller

Mr. & Mrs. Jeffrey C. Miritello

Mr. James C. Mitchell

Mr. & Mrs. Loren Mitchell

Mr. & Mrs. Robert H. Mitchell

Modesto Loan & Jewelry Co.

Montana Outfitters

Mr. Leslie Moore

Mr. Manuel D. Morais

Mr. Dominic J. Morin

Mr. & Mrs. Thomas C. Morrow

Mr. David W. Myers

Mr. Selim Nahas

Mr. Christopher Neely

Mr. William H. Neth, II

Mr. Robert D. Nichols

Mr. & Mrs. Ruben C. Nolf

Dr. Willard Noyes

Mr. & Mrs. David W. Nunnally

Mr. & Mrs. Harold C. O'Connor

Mr. Richard O'Connor

Mr. Mack O'Neal

Mr. & Mrs. Robert W. Obreiter

Mr. & Mrs. Milt Ocumpaugh

Old Fontenelle Gun Shop

Mr. Anthony J. Orlando

Mr. Larry Orr

Mr. & Mrs. Arlan L. Otto

Mr. Eldon J. Owens

Mr. & Mrs. David Packard

Mr. Calvin Patrick, Sr.

Mr. & Mrs. Larry M. Pedersen

Mr. & Mrs. Severen Pedersen

Mr. & Mrs. Al Perry

Mr. Ronald C. Petersen

Mr. and Ms. J. C. Peterson

Mr. Gary L. Petrek

Mr. Kermit Rex Plough

Mr. & Mrs. Ralph Pond

Pony Express Sport Shop, Inc.

Mr. & Mrs. Lamar Poole

Mr. Charles L. Porter

Dr. & Mrs. Hubert M. Porter

Mr. Thomas A. Porter

Mr. Allen Postel

Mr. Tim Powell

Mr. & Mrs. Edward L. Prater

Mr. Joe Prather

Mr. Leland L. Pratt

Mr. & Mrs. G. Thomas Puett

Mr. & Mrs. Raymond L. Pylant

Mr. Gary W. Quinlan &
  Mr. Dale Troutman

Mr. Roger F. Quisenberry

Mr. & Mrs. Wilburn J. Raithel

Mr. Ron Ramerth

Mr. Ronald J. Rando

Mr. Gerald Randrup

Mr. Robert E. Reabe

Mr. Bill Rebovich

Mr. Robert C. Renneberg

Mr. Gary H. Reynolds

Mr. & Mrs. Tommy L. Rholes

Mr. Ron Ricard

Mr. Duane Richards

Mr. David E. Riffle

Mr. Ray Rink

Mr. James R. Rising

Mr. Frank Roberts

Mr. Gary L. Robertson

Mr. & Mrs. Eugene A. Rodowicz

Mr. Robert W. Rohrig

Mr. Murray R. Roth

Mr. & Mrs. Delmar Rozeboom

Mr. Robert G. Ruben

Mr. Henry A. Rudkin, Jr.

Mr. & Mrs. Ivan Rumsey

Mr. & Mrs. Nicholas G. Rutgers, Jr.

Mr. & Mrs. Ty Rutledge

Mr. & Mrs. Ray Saign

Mr. Joseph L. Salter

Dr. Wallace Salter

Mr. Kurt H. Saxon

Mr. Hans W. Schemke

Mr. & Mrs. Konrad F. Schreier, Jr.

Mr. Jack Schubert

Mr. & Mrs. Bob G. Schulz

Mr. & Mrs. Rodney E. Schwartz

Mr. & Mrs. Pete Scripps

Mr. & Mrs. Jim Shannon

Mr. & Mrs. Randy S. Shuman

Mr. Mike Simens

Mr. & Mrs. Billy E. Simons

Mr. C. W. Slagle

Mr. Courtney C. Smith

Mr. David W. Smith

Mr. & Mrs. Harlan V. Smith

Mr. & Mrs. Larry L. Smoot

Mr. & Mrs. Malcolm R. Sneddon

Mr. Jon M. Solem

Mr. Paul Sorrell

Mr. Bruce W. Spaulding

Mr. Langford Spraggins

Dr. Donald A. Spring, M.D.

Mr. & Mrs. Edward B. Stabler

Mr. & Mrs. Lewis T. Steadman

Mr. Ernest E. Stinsa

Mr. Thomas E. Stratton, Jr.

Mr. & Mrs. Robert L. Strauss

Mr. Richard S. Taylor

Mr. William B. Telford &
  Ms. Elizabeth L. Murray

Mr. Gerald D. Tomac

Mr. Doug Turnbull

Mr. & Mrs. Donald Tusher

Mr. Tim A. Tyler

Mr. Erick Umphress

Mr. & Mrs. Thurston VanHorn

Mr. William Van Horn

Mr. Thomas J. Vetri

Mr. Jeffery Vidal

Mr. & Mrs. Harry L. Viezens

Mr. Kenneth Alan Vosburgh

Mr. & Mrs. Vern Vossler

Mr. Jim Voulgaris

Mr. Jim Waldon

Mr. Frederick Wallace

Mr. & Mrs. John C. Wallace

Mr. Steve Walters

Mr. & Mrs. Leon E. Wandler

Mr. & Mrs. Roy D. Warren

Mr. Brad Watkins

Mr. and Ms. V. M. Watt, Jr.

Mr. & Mrs. Walter J. Webb

Mr. Michael E. Welch

Mr. Monty Whitley

Mr. William Widner

Mr. Allen Wilson

Mr. & Mrs. Hugh M. Winderweedle, Jr.

Mr. Stuart Wright

Mr.Christopher J. Yuhas